Religion from the Inside

European Academy of Religion (EuARe) Lectures

EuARe Executive Committee:
Karla Boersma, Francesca Cadeddu, Jocelyne Cesari,
Alessandro Ferrari, Hans-Peter Grosshans,
Pantelis Kalaitzidis, Peter Petkoff,
Herman J. Selderhuis, Kristina Stoeckl

Volume 6

EUROPEAN
ACADEMY OF
RELIGION

Religion from the Inside

Sixth Annual Conference 2023

Edited by
Herman J. Selderhuis

DE GRUYTER

ISBN 978-3-11-145463-4
e-ISBN (PDF) 978-3-11-145465-8
e-ISBN (EPUB) 978-3-11-145505-1
ISSN 2940-455X
DOI https://doi.org/10.1515/9783111454658

Library of Congress Control Number: 2024941820

Bibliographic information published by the Deutsche Nationalbibliothek
The Deutsche Nationalbibliothek lists this publication in the Deutsche Nationalbibliografie; detailed bibliographic data are available on the internet at http://dnb.dnb.de.

Typesetting: Integra Software Services Pvt. Ltd.

www.degruyter.com

Contents

Introduction —— VII

David Brown
Enlightenment, the Kenotic Christ and Revelation from the Inside —— 1

John Makransky
Buddhist Constructive Reflection Past and Present: Recurrent Reinterpretation in Meeting New Cultural Needs and Challenges —— 21

Lejla Demiri
An Islamic Approach to Islamic Studies? Muslim Faith Commitment in the European Orientalist Sphere —— 43

Diwakar Acharya
Knowing and Thinking about the Ultimate in Hindu Theology: The Issues of Transcendence and Immanence —— 61

Index —— 77

Introduction

In this sixth volume in the series EUARE LECTURES readers will find the lectures presented at the European Academy of Religion's Sixth Annual Conference as it took place on June 19–23, 2023 at the University of St Andrews. The conference was co-organized by the *St Andrews Encyclopaedia of Theology* (SAET) and hosted jointly by the SAET and the Australian Catholic University. I'm happy to take the opportunity of this introduction to express my gratitude to the team at St. Andrews under the leadership of Brendan Wolfe and Sterlin Yates. I wish this volume could enclose the great organizational setting and the impressive hospitality all participants enjoyed while in St. Andrews.

The theme 'Religion from the Inside' was explored across five keynote addresses – four of which are published here – and more than 130 panels in which the question was dealt with how the existence of emic knowledge can be an invitation and a stimulus to academic exploration. Religion as object of research demands the awareness of the peculiarities of religion as having a fundamental impact on individuals, not to mention the impact on societies, history, world views etc. 'Religion from the Inside' was not chosen out of the conviction that you need to be religious to do religious studies, but to discuss whether knowledge about or even experience of the 'lived religion' can enrich religious studies. Those inside religion might see academic rationality as a problem and a threat to their religion, but does this imply that scholars should stay outside religion or that those engaged in religion should stay away or even be kept away from the academy? The highly intellectual philosophical and theological traditions originating from the late medieval Christian monasteries are good proof that it can be very fruitful to connect inside and outside. And the examples from various religions given by the keynote lecturers at St. Andrews confirm just this.

The papers in this volume deal with this question that is how to make use of the inside without losing the outside. They approach the question and come up with answers from various religious and academic perspectives, and each one of these papers is a treasure for further reflection and deserves close reading. Religions are ways of life and have characteristics that are not easy to grasp if only looked at from the outside. This implies that any research leaving these characteristics out as being irrelevant or unacademic misses essential elements for a good academic result. It's like talking about soccer without ever having played soccer. The topic of the conference at the same time demanded awareness of the challenges for scholars in religious studies adhering to a religion themselves to keep the distance needed for a solid academic approach of their own religion or that of others. Soccer players do have field experience but to perform well or even better they need the perspective from those at the sideline. This means – and the lec-

https://doi.org/10.1515/9783111454658-203

tures here published give evidence of that in various examples – the need for interdisciplinarity and the urgent need for the inclusion of non-Western perspectives but even more so the need for cooperation between the academic world of religious studies and the non-academic world of religion. Scholars in religious studies will profit from not only knowing about religious texts, traditions, and convictions but also by interacting with these texts and with those engaged in the theologies of these texts. In short: etic needs emic. This opens up new perspectives, asks for new methodologies, and demands a farewell to the wall between 'us' in academia and 'them' in religion. What is needed is a dialogue. The European Academy of Religion aims at stimulating and facilitating that dialogue and this volume will certainly contribute to that objective.

Herman Selderhuis

David Brown

Enlightenment, the Kenotic Christ and Revelation from the Inside

1 Introduction

In this essay I offer a defence of 'Religion from the Inside' but in a way which is perhaps somewhat unusual. I shall start from the opposite extreme, in the eighteenth-century movement known as the Enlightenment, noting some of its principal concerns. However, whereas its advocates thought that they had two decisive arguments against any attempt at religion from the inside, I shall argue that the Enlightenment approach to history actually effectively secured its own demise, once serious consideration is given to what the historical method disclosed about the actual nature of the biblical text. Instead of individual isolated judgements being the appropriate norm, kenosis reveals a developing, contextualised story that needs to be told both about Jesus and his disciples' response to him. The final section of the lecture then applies this insight, first to how other religions might be regarded, and then to a changed assessment of the relative weighing of the various subdisciplines in the study of religion. So I begin with the Enlightenment, whose antecedents are found in seventeenth century figures such as René Descartes but whose main flourishing was undoubtedly during the eighteenth century, symbolically ending perhaps in 1804 in the collapse of the French Revolution under Napoleon's imperial ambitions.[1]

2 Enlightenment

Much contemporary theological writing continues to find nothing positive in Enlightenment thought, portraying it as a bout of excessively rationalist writing that was entirely destructive in its consequences.[2] But, as contemporary historians are increasingly acknowledging, much of the impetus for the movement came from

1 Descartes (1596–1650) offered a model for future 'cold' rationalism. The French Revolution initially adopted the values of the Enlightenment, some of which were challenged by Napoleon. Although he had already become First Consul in 1799, his transition to Emperor is a good date to mark the movement's closure since Immanuel Kant also died that same year.

2 It is, for example, a recurring theme in the writings of the English theologian, Colin Gunton (1941–2003).

https://doi.org/10.1515/9783111454658-001

clergy and Christians more generally, in a revolt against superstition and towards the creation of a more ordered world, in everything from agriculture to hygiene. As Bill Jacobs observes in *The Oxford History of Anglicanism* "in England the Enlightenment was a predominantly Christian, Anglican and clerical phenomenon."[3] Equally, here in Scotland it would be a mistake to take David Hume as typical of the Scottish Enlightenment.[4] Hugh Blair, Adam Ferguson, Francis Hutcheson, William Robertson, and Adam Smith all display sympathy towards religion.[5] And among its results were the first modern attempts to produce more carefully researched and balanced accounts of past history, as with Hume, Gibbon, Herder, Robertson and Voltaire. Although the result was initially Lessing's famous "ugly ditch" between the eternal truths of reason and what he saw as the inadequately justified historical claims of Christianity,[6] and exaggerated late dating for New Testament texts from Reimarus onwards,[7] those earlier false starts did initiate a process that was eventually to witness more careful results that took us into the twentieth century with source, form, redaction and canonical criticism. The result has been a study of the scriptures which takes seriously the way in which human beings have helped to give decisive shape to their structure as we now have them.

Where, however, the Enlightenment's influence remained hostile was in the continued unwillingness of such scholars to speak of any active role for the divine. In large part this was perceived as a consequence of the search for objectivity, but no less pertinent was puzzlement about what might replace the once fashionable dictation model, re-affirmed in Pope Leo XIII's later incisive claim about the bible that "all the books and the whole of each book . . . were written at the dictation of the Holy Spirit,"[8] for it now looked as though the definitive contributing factor was purely human reflection. Indeed, it was a notion already enshrined in the earliest stages of Enlightenment thinking, in the common argument

---

3 W. M. Jacob, "England," in *The Oxford History of Anglicanism*, ed. Jeremy Gregory (Oxford: Oxford University Press, 2017), 96. The editor takes a similar view; cf. 20.

4 'Here' because the essay was originally delivered as a lecture at the University of St Andrews, Scotland in 2023.

5 See further Alexander Broadie, *The Scottish Enlightenment* (Edinburgh: Birlinn, 2007), sec. 5.

6 "The accidental truths of history can never become the proof of necessary truths of reason:" Gotthold Ephraim Lessing, *Lessing's Theological Writings*, trans. Henry Chadwick (London: A & C Black, 1956), 51–6, esp. 53; Gotthold Ephraim Lessing, *Lessings Werke*, ed. Kurt Wölfel, vol. 2, *Schriften I Schriften zur Poetik Dramaturgie Literaturkritik* (Frankfurt am Main: Insel Verlag, 1967), 307–12. He follows a distinction made by Origen in *Contra Celsum* (1.2) on the basis of I Cor. 2:5, that between prophecy and miracle.

7 The fragments of H. S. Reimarus were edited by Lessing in the decade following his death in 1768. That way, he went on to influence David Friedrich Strauss among others.

8 In the encyclical *Providentissimus Deus* of 1893 (my trans.).

that a deist, non-interventionist God was the only way divine justice could be defended, since otherwise the deity would be seen to be favouring one community of belief over another. Look up original sin, for instance, in Voltaire's *Philosophical Dictionary* and you will find him objecting to the doctrine as "a slander" of "the author of nature" in its unfairness, "created by the heated brain of a debauched and now repentant African" (his way of describing Augustine).[9] Still worse on Voltaire's view was the arbitrariness of the Christian doctrine of grace. "God must act by general laws, eternal like himself," Voltaire declares; "otherwise, he will seem like an insane master who gives wages to one slave and refuses nourishment to another."[10] Lessing took very much the same view, as indeed did his Jewish contemporary, Moses Mendelssohn.[11]

In observing such patterns of argument, it is important to note that for most Enlightenment thinkers these considerations were not supposed to lead to atheism but rather to a more chastened, more reasonable, form of religious belief. Thus, it is no accident that William Paley's defence of the argument from design dates from this period.[12] Evidences of divine existence, it was maintained, were universally available to all in the natural world. While it is a position which in the case of some did conceal non-belief, it would be quite wrong to suppose this generally the case. When, for example, Denis Diderot revealed his own atheism, Voltaire quickly replied with the assertion of his own commitment to religious belief, not only with the type of justification just mentioned but also putting such a notion in the mouth of an Anglican cleric (like myself!), Dr Freind in his short essay of 1775 *Histoire de Jenni*. His years in England had apparently led him to the conviction that the Church of England should be seen as the ideal in religious moderation.[13] Equally, despite Lessing's ditch to which we referred a moment ago, Lessing's own stance was not to advocate the abandonment of belief. His famous parable of the three identical rings in his play *Nathan the Wise* of 1779 was intended to make this point quite clear. While the choice of a specific religion can

9 Under *Péché original*: Voltaire, *Dictionnaire Philosophique* (Paris: Flammarion, 1964), 310–1 (my trans.).

10 Views given under his discussion of '*Grace*': Voltaire, 215–7 (my trans.)

11 For Mendelssohn an exclusive religion cannot possibly be true, since God wishes equal blessings on his human creation. For a helpful discussion of his position overall, David Sorkin, *Moses Mendelssohn and the Religious Enlightenment* (London: Peter Halban, 1996).

12 The *Evidences for Christianity* of William Paley (1743–1805) dates from 1794 and his *Natural Theology* from 1802, not long before he died. His earlier writing had been concerned with moral and political philosophy. He only first turned to apologetics in 1790, with *The Truth of Scripture History*.

13 Diderot's volume was entitled *The Virtue of the Philosopher*. Voltaire spent the year 1726 to 1728 in England.

only be a purely subjective matter, the choice is still necessary in order to have some code to follow. Again, most contemporary commentators would challenge how Kant was once seen in nineteenth and early twentieth century presentations, as arguing for the complete marginalisation of religion. On the contrary, not only does the idea of God have a clear rationale in his system, at the more practical level the divine is also seen at work through what Kant calls "providence" and the "spirit."[14]

Perhaps such aspects could be said to reflect the fact that Kant is not a purely Enlightenment figure, and indeed that would seem confirmed by his admiration for Rousseau. Even so, he can perhaps continue to be seen as typically Enlightenment in his demotion of the emotional. Not that the movement ignored the emotions but characteristically their rationality continued to be questioned. Most obviously, this is so in the case of David Hume where it was scepticism that led to him giving them a central place rather than any inherent valuing of them in their own right.[15] Equally, despite the novels of Diderot and Voltaire and the plays of Lessing, none sought to grapple with the possibility that the affective imagination might be an alternative way of accessing truth.[16] Indeed, one might take this devaluing of the affective and emotional as indicative of the rationalist tradition more generally across the entire course of western history, inasmuch as for Plato at its inception the emotions and imagination were there to support reason but never to direct it, as in his tripartite division of the soul in the *Republic*. In seeing the extent of that demotion of the emotions and the imagination, a salutary example to take is the Englishman who offered the definitive response to deism in the eighteenth century, Bishop Joseph Butler in his *Analogy of Religion*. The formal structure of his argument is that scriptural revelation works essentially like revelation in nature. The transformation of Christ's resurrection, for instance, is paralleled in the dramatic transition from caterpillar to moth or butterfly. But when it comes to the question of emotion, he is clear this has no proper part in religion. When John Wesley came to preach in the bishop's first diocese in Bristol in 1739,

---

14 See e.g. Christopher Insole, *The Intolerable God: Kant's Theological Journey* (Grand Rapids: Eerdmans, 2016); *Kant and the Divine* (Oxford: Oxford University Press, 2020).

15 Despite his familiar declaration that "reason is, and ought only to be the slave of the passions" (*Treatise on Human Nature* II, 3.3), it is not an alternative rationality that Hume offers for the emotions but observations on how they function psychologically. While his discussion of morality in that same *Treatise* (Book 3) adopts different terminology ("sentiments"), there is still no claim that they provide an alternative form of access to truth.

16 Diderot's best-known novel is *The Nun* of 1796 (*La Religieuse*, a satire on forced religious vocation), Voltaire's *Candide* of 1759 (a response to the Lisbon earthquake of 1755). Lessing wrote several plays. Apart from *Nathan the Wise*, note should be taken of the tragedies *Miss Sara Sampson* and *Emilia Galotti*.

Butler observed to Wesley of his sermons: "the pretending to extraordinary revelations and gifts of the Holy Spirit is a horrid thing, a very horrid thing." This was then elaborated later in his Charge of 1751 to clergy at Durham, the final see he occupied, where he declared "any affectation of talking piously is quite nauseous."[17] In other words, emotion in religion is judged quite wrong, because the person is seen as acting beyond the control of reason.

It takes little reflection to see why both aspects that we have mentioned here (the demand for an impartial approach and the exclusion of any appeal to the affective imagination) are inimical to religion. Although a few in modern times have tried living within more than one religion, it would be true to say that the exercise is extremely challenging, so easily does an impartial approach collapse into a reductionist one.[18] Again, so much of religion is dependent on imagination and emotion: certain insights simply become impossible unless built upon predispositions towards corresponding emotional responses, such as awe in some situations, guilt in others, joy in yet more. Moreover, the spiritual classics of Christianity again and again speak of the need to deepen faith through entering affectively and imaginatively into the details of the life of Christ, in texts as varied as the medieval Pseudo-Bonaventure *Meditations* or the Counter-Reformation Ignatius Loyola's *Spiritual Exercises*.[19]

Yet, surprisingly well into the twentieth century theologians were still trying to answer Lessing's challenge by talking of the availability of universal truths through scripture. The theology of Wilhelm Hermann is an early twentieth century example, where appeal was made to a potentially universal experience of sharing in the same inner life as Jesus.[20] But the trend continued well into our own times. Both Hermann's student, Rudolf Bultmann, and Paul Tillich can be seen as engaging in precisely the same sort of exercise. So, with Bultmann we are urged to find universal existential truths in the gospel, while Tillich goes even further in suggesting that what matters is not the historical individual who was Jesus but "the Christ," the transformation of reality to which the gospels bear wit-

17 For a general discussion of Butler's attitudes on the matter, Christopher Cunliffe, "'The Spiritual Sovereign': Butler's Episcopate," in *Joseph Butler's Moral and Religious Thought*, ed. Christopher Cunliffe (Oxford: Clarendon Press, 1992), 37–61, esp. 43–4, 56.

18 The phenomenon has been most conspicuous in the Christian Ashram movement. An early precedent was the seventeenth century Italian Jesuit, Roberto de Nobili. The most famous twentieth century example was the Benedictine priest, Bede Griffiths (1906–93).

19 The word 'imagine' is repeatedly used in both texts. There are many editions of the *Spiritual Exercises*. For Pseudo-Bonaventure: I. Ragusa and R. B. Green, eds., *Meditations on the Life of Christ* (Princeton, NJ: Princeton University Press, 1961).

20 Hermann died in 1922.

ness.[21] Such assumptions were reinforced by the conviction that historical conclusions should be like the truths of reason, easily accessible, with no age seen as fundamentally different from any other, as Ernst Troeltsch so strongly emphasised at the end of the nineteenth century.[22] Grand theory was to be avoided, with even major secular scholars like the Tudor historian Sir Geoffrey Elton insisting that the historian's task amounted to no more than the recreation of the particulars of the past.[23]

Ironically, depending on how one interprets the text,[24] perhaps the best alternative way forward is provided by one of Lessing's own late writings, his *Education of Humankind.*[25] For there Lessing does appear to take seriously the possibility that, instead of true knowledge being dependent on the instantaneous and universally accessible, truth might actually emerge through a more circuitous route, through a continuing narrative of change and interaction. More famously, it was also a position adopted by John Henry Newman in the nineteenth century in his *Essay on the Development of Doctrine*. "In another world it is otherwise; but here below to live is to change and to be perfect is to have changed often."[26] Yet, although Newman did thereby postulate a more complex, imaginative story for the development of doctrine and worship in the history of the later church, he fought shy of any suggestion that a similar pattern might be detectable within scripture itself. So let me now turn to the second part of my lecture, and indicate why thanks to the history of biblical scholarship, despite its reluctance to go beyond the objectivity of the particular, we can detect a similar pattern applying to the gospels in the notion of a kenotic Christ. Not only that, we will find answers to the two Enlightenment challenges mentioned earlier: that of unfairness in specific revelation, and the alleged impossibility of discovering the truth through the affective imagination.

---

21 Paul Tillich, *Systematic Theology*, vol. 2, *Existence and the Christ* (London: SCM, 2012), 107.

22 In his essay of 1898, Ernst Troeltsch, "Über historische und dogmatische Methode der Theologie," in *Gesammelte Schriften*, vol. 2 (Tübingen: Mohr/Paul Siebeck, 1913), 729–53.

23 See further G. R. Elton, *The Practice of History* (London: Fontana, 1967).

24 Henry Chadwick takes a less positive view than myself in his Introduction to the edition of Lessing mentioned earlier.

25 *Die Erziehung des Menschengeshlechts* of 1780: Lessing, *Lessings Werke*, 2:544–63.

26 John Henry Newman, *Essay on Development of Doctrine*, ed. J. M. Cameron (Harmondsworth: Penguin, 1973), 1.1., 100.

3 The Kenotic Christ

Because Christianity believed that its revelation disclosed a person who was both human being and God, the issue of kenotic or divine "self-emptying" has been there right from the beginning, with the notion given classic expression in an early letter of Paul, his Epistle to the Philippians: "Christ Jesus, though he was in the form of God . . . emptied himself, taking the form of a slave, being born in human likeness."[27] However, although the terminology has certainly been there right from the start, it is not true that its theological presentation has assumed the same conceptual form throughout. Patristic and medieval Christian thought in fact operated with a strong play on the two natures, Christ now acting in a human form and now in a divine, with the human a kenotic holding back of the divine nature to allow the lesser reality to present itself.

This led to some strange scenarios. For example, Athanasius can write: "Whether he wept or was troubled, the Logos or Word as such did not weep nor was he troubled, because that belongs to the flesh. If he prayed that the chalice might pass him by, it was not his divinity that experienced anguish but his human nature."[28] Sometimes mistranslations of the Hebrew helped in advancing this type of approach. In the second half of the first verse of Psalm 22 the Septuagint and Vulgate continued after "My God, my God. why have you forsaken me?" with the words, "far from my salvation, the words of my sins." The result was Augustine's suggestion that the cry of dereliction was not Christ speaking on his own behalf but on behalf of his sinful body, the Church.[29] Equally, in order to ensure the unity of the two natures, Aquinas insists on the availability to the human nature of infused knowledge, such that even in infancy Jesus knew his mission, including his eventual death and resurrection. The result is some otherwise very puzzling Renaissance paintings: Jesus, for example, pricking his finger on a thorn and realising what this foretold, or, more indirectly, engaging with a goldfinch, known for its predilection for thistle seeds.[30] So it is important to note that, though the language of kenosis was used, it was usually intended quite differently from how we might use such language today.[31]

What forced a different approach in the modern world was partly the rise of psychology and so the desire for a more adequate account of a unified consciousness in Christ that avoided this constant split between divine and human. But also, and more importantly here, there were the consequences of biblical criti-

27 Phil. 2:5–11 esp. 5–7 (RSNV).
28 Athanasius, *Patrologia Graeca*, 26, 249 (my trans.).
29 Augustine, *Exposition on the Psalms* 37.6.
30 E.g. in Raphael's *Madonna del Cardellino* (1596), now in the Uffizi, Florence.
31 There are some patristic exceptions, notably among Antiochene theologians.

cism. For most of Christian history Matthew and John had been the two gospels most read, both in the official liturgies of the church and privately. Mark was scarcely noticed because it was treated either as an abbreviation of Matthew, or else at most concerned with Jesus' actions rather than his teaching. However, historical criticism now argued that it was the earliest and as such operated with a significantly less exalted Christology than is to be found in the other three. For some, of course, the priority of Mark was seen to provide the historical heart of Jesus' ministry and all else was now portrayed as illegitimate elaboration. According to major figures such as David Friedrich Strauss, Auguste Renan and Adolf von Harnack, that is where Enlightenment principles of scholarship must lead us. But for most Christians something vital was seen as missing: that, however it was mediated, Jesus constituted in himself the definitive disclosure of who God really was.

But how could such a view still be defended? A surprising number of contemporary Christians still think that the only way to do this is by responding to the Enlightenment challenge on its own terms. So they insist on the historicity of the later, more substantial claims attributed to Jesus. Indeed, one might describe nineteenth-century fundamentalism (as, for example, it is embodied in the Princeton School) as simply a mirror image of the Enlightenment attitude to history. It continued to ignore any appeal to the imagination and instead insists on a literal fact embodied in those contested verses.[32] But, fortunately, a quite different alternative is available, to go beyond such assumptions into a defence of engaged imaginative truth as it works through the actual consequences of the inevitable conditioning of all thought and the gradualism this implies.

Take the implications of conditioning first. The Enlightenment had assumed that everyone has equal access to truth, in particular the truths of reason, whereas what historical research suggests is the heavily conditioned character of all thought. For better or worse, we are stuck in particular perspectives that are not easily dislodged. The current black woke agenda, for example, despite the issues being canvased often before, failed to find sufficient traction until our own time, so deeply embedded in the British case were convictions about the rightness of empire. Indeed, one can use the Enlightenment itself to indicate how tied human beings are to existing social norms. Even an intellectual genius like Kant, in common with most of the rest of his culture, thought that non-white races

32 Fundamentalism in its modern stress on the inerrancy of Scripture and certain other cardinal principles only really stems from the late nineteenth and early twentieth century, and in particular from the work of B. B. Warfield at Princeton Seminary.

were inferior, as were also women.[33] Rather than talking of "the scandal of particularity" in the incarnation as though this required some kind of defence,[34] it needs, therefore, to be asserted instead that it is in fact part of a general pattern, with here no less than elsewhere God needing to work, if at all, through the contingencies and limitations of history. Recognising as much enables us to answer the Enlightenment objection that God was unjust to choose one group over another. In fact, God *could not do anything otherwise* (my italics), if the divine patterns in creation were to be respected, not least this universal scenario of social conditioning. Truth can only emerge gradually through one particular history of social context rather than another. As we shall see later, this does not imply that only one religion is true, only that whatever truth emerges will be relative to a particular history and context.

But, in the meantime, let us explore the gospels, and see how it was only gradually that Jesus' disciples came to realise his full significance. Only at the resurrection did they finally move towards a particular assessment of who he was.[35] It took time and the right set of circumstances. Sometimes arguments to that effect are quite complicated, as in Wolfhart Pannenberg's claim in *Jesus: God and Man* that Jesus by anticipating the end of the age in his resurrection thereby demonstrated his identity with God.[36] More simply, though, we might talk of the resurrection events in themselves forcing the disciples towards such a conclusion. They had already seen Jesus' closeness to God in his lifetime, in the authority of his teaching, in his offer of forgiveness in God's name, and in the intimacy of his prayer and miracles. Now, this was confirmed in their experience of the resurrection. So many of the functions of God were seen as mediated through Christ that *function in effect became ontology* (my italics), preparing the way for the settlement of the early church councils.

Contrast such a progressive development with traditional Christian assumptions. For most of Christian history it had been assumed that anticipation of the ultimate Christian position was already firmly embedded in early material. Even the Trinity was found in the opening chapters of Genesis.[37] Such a backward pro-

33 For attitudes to race, including those of Kant, Emmanuel Chukwudi Eze, ed., *Race in the Enlightenment: A Reader* (Oxford: Blackwell, 1997). Although the majority view remains that Kant did not think highly of women, some female scholars have recently argued that he had a more nuanced view e.g. Mari Mikkole, "Kant on Moral Agency and Women's Role," in *Kantian Review* 16, no. 1 (March 2011): 89–111.

34 The phrase was popularised by the missiologist, Lesslie Newbigin (1909–98).

35 "And even then some still doubted:" Matt. 28:17.

36 W. Pannenberg, *Jesus: God and Man* (London: SCM, 1968; German, 1964).

37 E.g. in the use of the plural in Gen. 1:26: 'Let us make humankind in our image.'

jection was also endorsed by the New Testament itself, with for example Matthew's sometimes strange use of Old Testament prophecies, or the Epistle to the Hebrews speaking of Abraham's belief in the resurrection as the reason for his willingness to offer Isaac when no such belief existed either at the time the scene was set nor when that part of scripture was probably first written.[38]

But can the same scenario be postulated of Jesus himself? The language of kenosis is well-nigh universal in modern theology but with often markedly different metaphysics behind the same use of the word. Such questions do not need to be pursued here. More important is the implied recognition of development in Jesus' consciousness, as with the rest of us. As you are probably aware, New Testament scholars are currently engaged in what has been called the third quest of the historical Jesus. The first ended with Albert Schweitzer's mocking challenge to nineteen century German liberalism.[39] The second quest found the issue renewed in German scholars such as Ernst Käsemann and Günther Bornkamm.[40] Now we are into the third, with a conservative such as Tom Wright at one extreme and the radical Jesus Seminar at the other.[41] Standing in the middle is the recently deceased American John Meier who has written more on the topic than anyone else.[42]

However, secondary to the details of who is right is the more important consensus that Jesus must now be seen as part of a conditioned story. Yet, although he worked within an inheritance, he also sought to make it distinctively his own, as he interacts with those around him. So, while almost certainly his ministry was set in motion by the eschatological teaching of John the Baptist, he is surprisingly reticent about following one particular model, as in his rejection of Peter's description of him as a certain kind of Messiah,[43] his treatment of the exalted Son of Man as distinct from himself,[44] or again the title 'King of the Jews' never explicitly

38 Heb. 11:17–9.

39 "A figure designed by rationalism, endowed with life by liberalism and clothed by modern theology in an historical garb": Albert Schweitzer, *The Quest of the Historical Jesus: From Reimarus to Wrede* (London: A&C Black, 1911), 396.

40 Initiated by Ernst Käsemann (d. 1998) in 1953, it is principally associated with the work of Günther Bornkamm (d. 1990) in his *Jesus von Nazareth* (1956).

41 The term was first used by N. T. Wright in his updating of Stephen Neill and Tom Wright, *The Interpretation of the New Testament: 1861– 1986*, 2nd ed. (Oxford: Oxford University Press, 1988), 397.

42 For the latter, John P. Meier, *A Marginal Jew: Rethinking the Historical Jesus*, 5 vols. (New Haven: Yale University Press, 1991–2016). He was in the process of writing a sixth volume when he died in 2022.

43 Mark 8:27–33.

44 E.g. Mark 8:38; Matt. 10:32–3.

accepted.[45] But it is not just Peter's proposed definition that is rejected, equally Jesus is seen as rebelling against the advice of his family, or again against James's and John's wish to see themselves on thrones in a future world.[46] Equally, Matthew makes it clear that Jesus did not envisage the inclusion of the Gentiles in his own lifetime.[47] Yet thanks to Mark, there survives the story of the exchange with the Syro-Phoenican woman which suggests some movement on Jesus' part, even during his own lifetime. Indeed, this may well be why a record of this extraordinary encounter was preserved. The Gentile dogs, after all, do merit his concern.[48]

So, in short, there is both conditioning and a pushing back against its restraints but in a way that clearly demonstrates Jesus' own self-estimation and that of the disciples developing across the gospel story as a whole: a kenotic 'self-emptying' that refuses immediate answers, a being whom Christians have traditionally identified with the divine but who in all probability did not use that description for himself, instead identifying wholly with the human condition during his earthly life, Indeed, according to the conservative Catholic theologian Hans Urs von Balthasar, his Father may well have allowed him to be deceived, in common with so many of his contemporaries, about the imminence of the end, precisely in order to give sufficient urgency to his preaching.[49] Equally, the synoptic portrayal of Gethsemane surely implies that he had not expected his life to end in this way, which of course makes the cry of dereliction from the cross all the more poignant, so powerfully taken up in Jürgen Moltmann's *The Crucified God*,[50] and in so many others, yet so hugely different from how Augustine had viewed exactly the same scene, as we have seen.

But, if such kenosis is true both in Jesus' own consciousness and in the reception of his words and deeds by the disciples, what then are we to make of John's Gospel, where a quite different story appears to be told? It is here that I come to the second element of my critique of Enlightenment approach to scripture, the failure to acknowledge any other form of truth than the historical. Honoré de Balzac (d.1850), in introducing his great novel series *La Comédie humaine* as a "history of moral behaviour," muses: "In order to deserve the praise to which every

45 E.g. John 18:32–8.
46 The request is attributed to their mother in Matthew: Matt. 20:20.
47 Matt. 10:5: "Go nowhere among the Gentiles." Balanced in Matthew by the beginning and end of his gospel, with Gentile *magoi* coming to worship the child (2:1–12) and Jesus's final instruction to "make disciples of all nations" (28:19).
48 Mark 7:24–30.
49 Hans Urs von Balthasar, *The von Balthasar Reader*, ed. Medard Kehl and Werner Löser (Edinburgh: T&T Clark, 1982), 127–32.
50 Jürgen Moltmann, *The Crucified God* (London: SCM, 1974; German, 1973).

artist must aspire, am I not bound to study the causes or central cause of these social facts, and discover the meaning hidden in the immense assembly of characters, emotions and events?"[51] In other words, for Balzac imaginative fiction has become an alternative, better way of disclosing the underlying, social and personal truths of his time. Not only does the imagination offer a more powerful, affective impact it also penetrate deeper into underlying psychological motivations. Nor does his English contemporary Charles Dickens (d. 1870) take a different view. The dreadful Dotheboys Hall and its headmaster Wackford Squeers never existed. Yet their moving depiction in Dickens' novel *Nicholas Nickleby* had the emotional power to persuade his contemporaries to act against related social ills. Though based on places Dickens had seen, his fictional account conveyed successfully and more affectively those underlying historical truths.[52]

But can we apply this same underlying insight to John's Gospel? I think we can. However, let me first remind you of the extent of the difference between John and the synoptics. It is not just long speeches contrasted with pithy sayings, there is also a significantly different narrative. For John, Christ remains in total control throughout, thus effectively contradicting the synoptics at various points. Gethsemane becomes a rhetorical question instead of a serious trial.[53] Christ knows the future throughout, including when and where Judas will betray him. Nor has he any need for someone else to carry his cross,[54] while his last words from that cross are not words of desolation but of complete triumph: 'all has been accomplished.'[55]

Suppose, however, instead of talking of conflict between the gospels we see John as really re-telling the narrative from the divine perspective, offering a theo-

---

51 My translation: Honoré de Balzac, *La Comédie humaine*, vol.1 (Paris: Gallimard, 1976), 7–20, esp. 11. For a more general discussion of types of truth available through fiction, see my David Brown, *Discipleship and Imagination: Christian Tradition and Truth* (Oxford: Oxford University Press, 2000), 344–84; also my forthcoming *Gospel as Work of Art: Imaginative Truth and the Open Text* (Grand Rapids: Eerdmans, 2024), esp. 78–105.

52 Dickens had visited Bowes Academy in County Durham in 1838, where the headmaster, William Shaw, had been prosecuted some years earlier (in 1823) for two boys' being blinded because of beatings and poor nutrition. The inspiration for Spike was the tombstone of a boy who had died while attending the school.

53 The original request not to drink the cup (Mk. 14:35–6) becomes merely a rhetorical question in John (18:11).

54 The role of the angel in Gethsemane is simply to confirm Christ's already existing intentions (12:27), as he knows everything in advance, including how Judas will betray him (13:1–3 & 18–30). The detachment of troops sent to arrest him even falls to the ground in his presence (18:6), while he himself proves to have the necessary strength to carry his own cross (19:17).

55 Instead of the cry of dereliction as in Mark (15:34) there are words of triumph (John 19:30). The common translation 'it is finished' fails to capture the full force of the Greek perfect tense.

logical rather than a purely historical account. Although this is a considerable over-simplification, we might talk of the synoptics developing a narrative through which the believer is allowed to enter more fully into the humanity of the situation, while John's development allows us to explore more fully what it might mean to speak of a divinely guided plan throughout. Imaginatively, for the practice of faith we need both perspectives, and so it would be quite wrong to preclude one (John) on historical grounds or the other (the synoptics) for being insufficiently theological. Thinking of an open, developing narrative has actually allowed one to endorse both perspectives. It is the totality that has given us access to the truth, not individual incidents on their own. So not only is the Enlightenment focus on the particular fact a mistake, complete objectivity is a false ideal, if we want to see reality in the round, as it were. And it is precisely the brilliance of John's imaginative rewriting that enable us to appreciate fully the significance of that kenotic totality.[56]

To see the point, consider how even in his first two chapters John reshapes the narrative of Jesus's life from the viewpoint of where its open narrative eventually reached after the resurrection, in the divine perspective from which that life ultimately stemmed. In chapter 1 at Christ' Baptism John the Baptist is made to declare, 'Here is the Lamb of God who takes away the sin of the world.' It is a proclamation that makes no sense whatsoever at this stage of the narrative but it is entirely comprehensible when seen from the story's ending, with Christ sacrificed on the cross like the Temple lambs.[57] Again, take John's first miracle in the following chapter, the wedding at Cana. If we focus on the historical question, whether it happened, we actually miss its main point which is that Jesus is offering us an abundance of new wine quite unlike the water of earlier dispensations. Apart from lots of symbolism within the story itself, John even hints at this in his very opening words, 'on the third day.' Hardly a literal temporal identifier; instead, a hint that what follows will provide the deeper meaning to the resurrection.[58] Closely follows the cleansing of the Temple. An older generation would have postulated two cleansings since John places his at the very beginning of Christ's ministry and the synoptics at its very end. But surely the underlying point is again obvious. John has deliberately subordinated historical accuracy to his desire for greater imaginative engagement on the part of his readers. Here is

---

56 This argument is developed more fully in Brown, *Gospel as Work of Art*, esp. 392–402.

57 John 1:29. John makes the date of Jesus' death parallel the Day of Preparation when the lambs would be killed in preparation for the Passover feast.

58 John 2:1. For further symbolism later in the narrative, note the six (imperfect) rather than seven water jars, and the absurd over-provision of wine, in modern terms between 120 and 180 gallons.

someone offering us a completely new beginning in which Christ will in some sense become our new Temple: 'Destroy this temple, and in three days I will raise it up.'[59]

This is not to say that anything goes. Throughout his gospel it is possible to identify how John builds on the synoptic tradition but he allows imagination to take over precisely because he is convinced that history alone cannot deliver the goods, as it were. The synoptics can show us the kenotic Christ identifying with us in joy and pain but not the transcendent reality that constitutes his now permanent availability to us. So he asks readers at the same time to look at matters from a quite different perspective, the eternal dimension that belongs to God alone. The affective imagination has granted access to a deeper level of truth. The story of the unfolding life can now be told internally from the perspective of the whole.

4 Revelation from the Inside

And so turning, therefore, to the third and final section of my lecture, we might ask what such a transformed understanding of Christian scripture and the narrative it offers of the incarnation might entail for two key issues of our own day: how the different religions might best view one another, and what this might imply for how religion is taught in the contemporary university.

On the first point, no longer should we think of directly comparing one religion with another, but rather in each case, how its open narrative is worked through towards an appropriate conclusion. It is the story of development that matters, not particular isolated judgments.

Consider Judaism in the first instance. Debate continues to rage over how much of its legal traditions stem from Moses on Mount Sinai. To quote an extreme example, the so-called Copenhagen school transfer the whole account to the second century BCE.[60] Again, others such as Mark S. Smith and Thomas Römer argue that in its earliest period Judaism is still moving very slowly beyond a Midian war god, perhaps originally seen as part of a pantheon in which Yahweh was still subordi-

59 John 2:19. The verse has no parallel in the synoptic accounts. Nonetheless, it had some historical basis, in accusations made by others against Jesus e.g. Mark 14:58.

60 So called because that is where their principal advocate, Thomas L. Thompson, teaches. For Thompson's rather extreme views, see Thomas L. Thompson, *The Bible in History: How Writers Create a Past* (London: Jonathan Cape, 1999).

nate to El.[61] While such claims could easily be seen as a threat to the Jewish faith, an alternative approach would again be to take the history of Judaism as a whole: that what matters is less when a particular belief arose and more how it forms part of an evolving tradition. Nor need that be seen as a suitable response only from a liberal Jew. Turn to the works of a rabbi in the Conservative tradition like Benjamin Sommer, and this is precisely the defence he offers.[62]

Again, consider the threat now posed to contemporary Hinduism by fundamentalism, in the riots that followed claims that neither the cow as sacred nor reincarnation have always been part of that religion.[63] Admittedly, only the Vedantic tradition has conventionally been described as revelation, as smurti ('what is heard,)'[64] and neither belief seems to be present there, nor indeed many of the gods who subsequently became prominent. But in response a story could be told of subsequent developments in such directions, and so of a religion to be assessed as a whole, rather than in its isolated parts. Likewise, in Mahayana Buddhism the Lotus Sutra even offers an explanation for why certain beliefs about the Buddha had to wait for the right moment. The answer given is found in appeal to the notion of what are called 'skilful means:' of truth always spoken in ways most appropriate to the particular recipients at that time. Several powerful analogies for such a practice are offered, including a story of partial truths told to children in order to encourage flight from a burning house, and even a version of what might be called the parable of the prodigal son.[65] The result is that a whole range of means of pursuing enlightenment could now be added, without them necessarily being seen as originally proposed by the historical Buddha.

I hasten to add that it can hardly be my role to judge the truth or falsity of any particular religion in relation to another. My point is simply that the wrong kind of judgment is being made if, as on the Enlightenment model, religious claims are assessed in isolation from the rest of its developing belief system. What matters is where it fits in the story of a developing tradition as a whole, and

---

61 Mark S. Smith, *The Origins of Biblical Monotheism* (Oxford: Oxford University Press, 2001), esp. 193–94; Thomas Römer, *The Invention of God* (Cambridge, MA: Harvard University Press, 2015), 24–85.

62 Benjamin Sommer, *Revelation and Authority: Sinai in Jewish Scripture and Tradition* (New Haven: Yale University Press, 2015), esp. 30–35. He teaches at the Jewish Theological Seminary of America, based in New York.

63 For the contention that Hindu culture was originally meat-eating, see Dwigendra Narayan Jha, *The Myth of the Holy Cow* (Delhi: Oxford University Press, 2004).

64 Rather than the weaker *sruti* (what is read).

65 In chapters 3 and 4 of *The Lotus Sutra,* trans., Gene Reeves (Somerville, MA: Wisdom Publications, 2008), 103–57. In the latter, the son is left to work on a dung heap until the right attitudes have been inculcated.

from that perspective it becomes possible even for a committed Christian like myself to concede that on the trajectory of that open narrative those other religions may have sometimes discovered something that Christianity as yet lacks. Indeed, to give a couple of examples almost at random, I would happily concede that Hinduism handles the imagery of sexuality within the divine better than my own faith, or again that Buddhism is more plausible in dealing with the issue of valuing transience.[66]

However, given that there is not the space here to pursue these complex issues, let me instead tackle a nearer faith, that of Islam and what it does with the traditions of Judaism and Christianity. Despite an initial impression of an unchanging deposit, here too it is possible to speak of change within an open narrative in a way that adherents of that faith might well be prepared to endorse, as in the different emphases between Meccan and Medinan sutras, or abrogation for other reasons such as some especially prominent hadith, or, more recently, arguments from analogy.[67] While no doubt non-believers will continue to explain such change in terms of purely human factors, there is no reason why the same revelatory principle as deployed by Christianity might not also be applied here: that the transcendent chooses to work within the confines of human conditioning in a way that guarantees appropriate inward reception of the message at one point rather than another.

Take a very particular example, Zachariah learning of the future role of his son, John the Baptist. In the original Lucan version Zachariah is struck dumb for not believing the angel's words,[68] whereas according to the Qur'anic revelation a three-day dumbness is requested by Zechariah as a sign that God would indeed accomplish what was being promised. Surely it is not a betrayal of the Christian faith to admit that it is the Qur'an that offers a less petty, more sympathetic account of divine motivation?[69] Zechariah is no longer punished for not believing what he might well have reasonably doubted.

And so to the final issue I said I would consider, the question of imagination and affective input, and in particular how this might contribute to how religion is taught in our universities. For too long, in pursuit of objectivity, certain disciplines have been excluded from the curriculum, among them the study of liturgy,

---

66 See further in David Brown, *Learning from Other Religions* (Cambridge: Cambridge University Press, 2024): my discussion of sexuality and divinity in ch. 3; my discussion of transience in ch. 6 (the section on 'Zen minimalism and impermanence').

67 The earlier Meccan sutras are shorter. For an example of hadith (oral tradition) abrogating, take Muslims praying five times a day. The Qur'an only mentions three: 24:58; 11:116.

68 Luke 1:20.

69 Qur'an 19:10.

spirituality, the role of music or relations between theology and the arts more generally. But don't they take us to the heart of what makes any particular religion 'tick,' as it were? To remind you of how far the malaise once went, let me bring to mind the distant past when I read Classics at the University of Edinburgh. I vividly recall enduring a whole year studying Aeschylus's *Agamemnon* when, in pursuit of objectivity, the only topics under consideration were such things as the precise date of a play and alternative textual readings. What was missing was any attention of what makes it a great play or why religious belief might be integral to its interpretation.[70] Fortunately, classics has now radically changed. But, sadly, theology and religious studies are still catching up. This is emphatically not to say that only believers can adequately teach a religious text.[71] But what is required is that lecturers, whether believers or not, enter imaginatively into that text, in order to see what it might have meant from the inside, and convey such feelings to their students: in other words, demonstrate what once made its message matter.

Just as I used the later Lessing to indicate how storied contextuality might be a better approach than isolated universal truths, so let me conclude here by drawing on a hymn writer from that period to show how appeal to emotion and the affective imagination need not totally undermine Enlightenment concerns. The twentieth century rightly witnessed a huge retreat from the imagery in nineteenth century hymns that spoke of believers being bathed in the blood of Christ, and quite rightly so. Not only was the imagery quite gruesome, it also allowed believers to indulge in emotion to the subordination of all other considerations.[72]

But not all appeals to the affective imagination are of that kind. The eighteenth-century Isaac Watts remains one of England's greatest hymn-writers.[73] In what is perhaps his greatest hymn, 'When I survey the wondrous cross,' he does not hesitate to describe that death in graphic terms, yet in a way that still insists

---

70 The lecturer interacted with the equally narrow common set text of the time: J. D. Dennison and Denys Page ed., *Aeschylus Agamemnon* (Oxford: Clarendon Press, 1957). This is not deny that a minority of classics scholars even at the time took a different approach: e.g. Gilbert Murray, *Aeschylus: The Creator of Tragedy* (Oxford: Clarendon Press, 1940). But it is only recent times that have seen an explosion of interest in underlying religious issues.

71 Though it is worth remembering that Christian have often been quite bad at empathising with the texts of other religions, a phenomenon observed as early as the objections raised by the Emperor Julian (361–3) to Christians teaching pagan texts.

72 E.g. E. A. Hoffman's 1878 hymn, "Have you been to Jesus for the cleansing power?" with its recurring line, "Are you washed in the blood of the Lamb?"

73 Other hymns by Watts (1674–1748) include 'Jesus shall reign, where'er the sun,' 'O God our help in ages past' and 'Joy to the world'.

that emotion and reason are judged both equally appropriate to how that death should be conceived. Consider first the third and fourth verses of the hymn:

> See from his head, his hands, his feet,
> Sorrow and love flow mingled down,
> Did e'er such love and sorrow meet,
> Or thorns compose so rich a crown?
>
> His dying crimson, like a robe,
> Spreads o'er his body on the tree;
> Then am I dead to all the globe,
> And all the globe is dead to me.[74]

I cannot help but hear the traditional accompanying music and so be profoundly moved.[75] Yet the imagery of the blood flowing like a king's robe does not overwhelm those singing the hymn or reflecting on its implications precisely because Watts had insisted in his opening line on observation from a distance: "survey" is his chosen term, not "inspect" (or "examine closely"). The gore can thus become beautiful, a symbol of "sorrow and love," precisely because a discrete distance has been maintained: simultaneously, cool Enlightenment reflection and real religious engagement. So, while we are thus left in no doubt about Christ's agony, the suffering is not allowed to destroy all other considerations. It is one of England's greatest hymns, and precisely because it refuses this divide between Enlightenment distance or objectivity and what pushes beyond, in a full engagement of the emotions.

It is this same balance that this lecture has been concerned to advocate, to encourage our students to see why religion matters so much, yet in a way that does not destroy their ability to arbitrate between rival positions. Religions live and breathe in their totalities, not in the isolated assessment of individual verses nor in the denigration of the imagination and emotion which alone can give religion its dynamism and life.

David Brown is Emeritus Wardlaw Professor of Theology, Aesthetics and Culture at the University of St Andrews and he is an ordained Anglican priest. His previous appointments were at Oxford and Durham. He has written extensively on the relations between theology and philosophy, and theology and the arts. Examples of the former are *The Divine Trinity* (1985) and *Divine Humanity: Kenosis and the*

74 J. R. Watson draws parallels with Ignatian spirituality: J. R. Watson, *An Annotated Anthology of Hymns* (Oxford: Oxford University Press, 2002), 135. For a more extended discussion, see J. R. Watson, *The English Hymn* (Oxford: Oxford University Press, 1997), 160–70.

75 The most common tune is Rockingham, itself based on a folk melody dating back to at least 1724.

Construction of a Christian Theology (2011); of the latter the five-volumed OUP series that began with *Tradition and Imagination: Revelation and Change* (1999). Two recent books are *Gospel as Work of Art: Imaginative Truth and the Open Text* (Eerdmans, 2024) and *Learning from Other Religions* (Cambridge University Press, 2024). He was elected a Fellow of the British Academy in 2002 and of the Royal Society of Edinburgh in 2012.

Bibliography

Augustine. *Exposition on the Psalms 37.6.*
Athanasius. *Patrologia Graeca*, 26., 249
Balthasar, Hans Urs von. *The von Balthasar Reader*. Edited by Merard Kehl and Werner Löser. Edinburgh: T&T Clark, 1982.
Balzac, Honoré de. *La Comédie humaine*. Vol. 1. Paris: Gallimard, 1976.
Broadie, Alexander. *The Scottish Enlightenment*. Edinburgh: Birlinn, 2007.
Brown, David. *Discipleship and Imagination: Christian Tradition and Truth*. Oxford: Oxford University Press, 2000.
Brown, David. *Gospel as Work of Art: Imaginative Truth and the Open Text*. Grand Rapids: Eerdmans, 2024.
Brown, David. *Learning from Other Religions*. Cambridge: Cambridge University Press, 2024.
Cunliffe, Christopher. "'The Spiritual Sovereign': Butler's Episcopate." In *Joseph Butler's Moral and Religious Thought*, edited by Christopher Cunliffe, 37–61. Oxford: Clarendon Press, 1992.
Dennison, J. D., and Denys Page, eds. *Aeschylus Agamemnon*. Oxford: Clarendon Press, 1957.
Elton, G. R. *The Practice of History*. London: Fontana, 1967.
Eze, Emmanuel Chuckwudi. *Race in the Enlightenment: A Reader*. Oxford: Blackwell, 1997.
Insole, Christopher. *The Intolerable God: Kant's Theological Journey*. Grand Rapids: Eerdmans, 2016.
Insole, Christopher. *Kant and the Divine*. Oxford: Oxford University Press, 2020.
Jacob, W. M. "England." In *The Oxford History of Anglicanism*, edited by Jeremy Gregory, 91–119. Oxford: Oxford University Press, 2017.
Jha, Dwigendra Narayan. *The Myth of the Holy Cow*. Delhi: Oxford University Press, 2004.
Lessing, Gotthold Ephraim. *Lessing's Theological Writings*. Translated by Henry Chadwick. London: Adam & Charles Black, 1956.
Lessing, Gotthold Ephraim. *Lessings Werke*. Vol. 2, *Schriften I Schriften zur Poetik Dramaturgie Literaturkritik*, edited by Kurt Wölfel. Frankfurt am Main: Insel Verlag, 1967.
The Lotus Sustra. Translated by Gene Reeves. Somerville, MA: Wisdom Publications, 2008.
Meier, John P. *A Marginal Jew: Rethinking the Historical Jesus*. 5 vols. New Haven: Yale University Press, 1991–2026.
Mikkola, Mari. "Kant on Moral Agency and Women's Role." *Kantian Review* 16, no. 2 (March 2011): 89–111.
Moltmann, Jürgen. *The Crucified God*. London: SCM, 1974; German, 1973.
Murray, Gilbert. *Aeschylus: The Creator of Tragedy*. Oxford: Clarendon Press, 1940.
Neill, Stephen, and Tom Wright. *The Interpretation of the New Testament: 1861–1986*. 2nd ed. Oxford: Oxford University Press, 1988.
Newman, John Henry. *Essay on Development of Doctrine*. Edited by J. M. Cameron. Harmondsworth: Penguin, 1973.
Pannenberg, W. *Jesus: God and Man*. London: SCM, 1968; German, 1964.

Ragusa, I., and R. B. Green. *Meditations on the Life of Christ*. Princeton, NJ: Princeton University Press, 1961.
Römer, Thomas. *The Invention of God*. Cambridge, MA: Harvard University Press, 2015.
Schweitzer, Albert. *The Quest of the Historical Jesus: From Reimarus to Wrede*. London: A&C Black, 1911.
Smith, Mark S. *The Origins of Biblical Monotheism*. Oxford: Oxford University Press, 2001.
Sommer, Benjamin. *Revelation and Authority: Sinai in Jewish Scripture and Tradition*. New Haven: Yale University Press, 2015.
Sorkinm, David. *Moses Mendelssohn and the Religious Enlightenment*. London: Peter Halban, 1996.
Thompson, Thomas L. *The Bible in History: How Writers Create a Past*. London: Jonathan Cape, 1999.
Tillich, Paul. *Systematic Theology*. Vol. 2, *Existence and the Christ*. London: SCM, 2012.
Troeltsch, Ernst. "Über historische und dogmatische Methode der Theologie." In *Gesammelte Schriften*. Vol. 2. Tübingen: Mohr/Paul Siebeck, 1913.
Voltaire. *Dictionnaire Philosophique*. Paris: Flammarion, 1964.
Watson, J. R., *An Annotated Anthology of Hymns*. Oxford: Oxford University Press, 2002.
Watson, J. R., *The English Hymn*. Oxford: Oxford University Press, 1997.

John Makransky

Buddhist Constructive Reflection Past and Present: Recurrent Reinterpretation in Meeting New Cultural Needs and Challenges

1 Introduction

This essay will discuss the rise of Buddhist constructive reflection (also called "Buddhist theology") in the modern academy, its two goals, and how analogues of its two goals have been operative throughout Buddhist history in Asia and the West – Buddhism newly informing each culture as it also being newly informed by it.[1] Some current applications of Buddhist constructive reflection in light of that history will be discussed, including ways that modern Buddhist thinkers are drawing on traditional Buddhist resources, together with contemporary academic disciplines and social and natural sciences, to address current questions and problems. As modern Buddhism makes new contributions in these ways, it also risks succumbing so much to modern assumptions and values that its ability to offer important alternatives to them is reduced. An example of this will also be noted. Although my focus here is on Buddhism, readers will see interesting parallels and differences with analogous theological developments in other religious traditions.

2 The Emergence of Buddhist Critical-Constructive Reflection (Buddhist Theology) in the Modern Academy

The modern academic study of religions (under the rubric of "religious studies" and "history of religions") analyzes how religious concepts and practices develop within historical and cultural contexts. This way of analyzing religions emerged in

1 See Roger Jackson "Buddhist Theology: Its Historical Context," and John Makransky, "Contemporary Academic Buddhist Theology: Its Emergence and Rationale" in *Buddhist Theology: Critical Constructive Reflections by Contemporary Scholars*, ed. Roger Jackson and John Makransky (New York: Routledge, 2000), 1–21.

https://doi.org/10.1515/9783111454658-002

the modern Western academy under the influence of the European enlightenment. Central to its emergence has been the method of "epoché" – avoiding judgments of normative truth and value in order to open a new space in the academy for the historical study of religions free from Christian judgments on non-Christian religions, and also free from pre-modern Christian assumptions about Christianity's own developments. In twentieth century Europe and the Americas, departments of religious studies, history of religions, and cultural studies (that include study of religions) were established in hundreds of universities, while university theology departments and seminaries remained the loci of Christian theological studies. Thus, an institutional separation was made between *religious studies* on the one hand and *theological studies* on the other.[2] Whereas religious studies scholars used historical and social analysis of religions *descriptively* as a source of data for modern *academic* theorization, Christian theologians like Karl Rahner, Paul Tillich, Johann Baptist Metz, Elizabeth Johnson, Gustavo Gutierrez, and Ivone Gebarra, used the same kinds of historical and social analysis for *normative* theological purposes, to see how such analyses could inform newly effective ways to understand, practice and apply truths of Christianity in the modern world.

By the 1980s and 90s, the institutional separation of religious studies from Christian theology had begun to unleash new kinds of interest in the academy. A number of non-Christian PhD students in religious studies programs wanted to apply the critical findings of the academy to clarify the truth and value of their own religious traditions in the current world from a critical-constructive perspective, as Christian theologians do. This included scholars of the various Asian traditions, prominently Buddhism, Hinduism, Confucianism, and Islam. But there was no ready-made academic location in the Western academy for such *non-Christian* theological work. The Western religious studies academy was dedicated to the descriptive study of religions, *not* normative religious reflection, while normative reflection was housed mainly in *Christian* theological institutions.

The interest in normative, critical religious reflection arose strongly in the Buddhist studies wing of the academy at the turn of this century, in part, because growing global interest in Buddhism included a *normative* concern to explore ways of drawing on Buddhism as a resource to help address modern questions and problems. Also in this period, a new generation of scholars doing PhDs in Buddhist studies, who also practiced Buddhism within Buddhist communities East and West, wanted to use academic disciplines to help clarify normative possibilities of their Buddhist traditions. In 2006, some of those Buddhist scholars es-

2 See Gregory Alles, "Study of Religion: An Overview," in *Encyclopedia of Religion*, 2nd ed., vol. 13 ed. Lindsay Jones (Detroit: Macmillan Reference, 2005), 8761–8767.

tablished a new area of study in the American Academy of Religion dedicated to Buddhist critical-constructive reflection, which has also been called "Buddhist theology," since it represents a new niche in the academy for combining modern critical analysis of a tradition with normative reflection upon it, as academic theologians do.

3 Two Goals of Buddhist Critical-Constructive Reflection (BCR)

Buddhist critical-constructive reflection has had two goals: To reflect critically on aspects of Buddhism in light of contemporary understandings, and to reflect critically on contemporary understandings in light of Buddhism. The first goal involves drawing on modern academic disciplines, together with Buddhist understandings, to newly inform aspects of Buddhism in normative ways. The second goal involves drawing on Buddhism to address contemporary problems and needs and to newly inform current areas of knowledge, such as philosophy, psychology, ecology, cognitive science, and economics. Thus, while academic work in religious studies is primarily etic and descriptive, Buddhist critical-constructive reflection draws on those etic findings, together with emic Buddhist understandings, to suggest new normative directions for Buddhism, society and academia.[3] Henceforth I will refer to Buddhist critical-constructive reflection as BCR for ease of expression. While the focus here is on BCR, academic theological work by scholars of other non-Christian religious traditions has also been growing in recent decades.

3.1 The First Goal of BCR: Drawing On Contemporary Understandings to Inform Buddhism

How did I become involved in this recent development in the academy? The need for new normative Buddhist reflection first occurred to me as a PhD student, when I read an essay by Donald Lopez, a Buddhist studies scholar who maintains

3 See Roger Jackson and John Makransky, eds. *Buddhist Theology: Critical Reflections by Contemporary Buddhist Scholars*, (Surrey, England: Curzon Press, 2000), for an early collection of essays exploring the discipline of Buddhist critical-constructive reflection. On problems and possibilities entailed constructing the discipline of religious studies in relation to religious traditions and theologies, see José Cabezon, "The Discipline and its Other: The Dialectic of Alterity in the Study of Religion," *Journal of the American Academy of Religion* 74, no. 1 (March 2006): 21–38.

the religious studies posture of restricting himself to descriptive analysis of religions, while avoiding normative concerns. I'll note some of the historical background assumed in Lopez's essay before discussing that essay.

Generally speaking, religious change has *not* been valued in Asian Buddhist cultures. For traditional Asian Buddhists, if Buddhist understandings and practices were seen to have changed significantly over time in new cultural contexts, it would signify that they had fallen away from the original teaching of Shakyamuni Buddha.[4] Given that non-historicizing assumption, Asian Buddhists have used various strategies to establish legitimacy for new Buddhist developments in cultures, while hiding their newness. One such strategy involved use of the Buddhist doctrine of skillful means (*upāya-kauśalya*), which, in one principal meaning, refers to the pedagogical methods Śākyamuni Buddha used to meet the differing mentalities of individuals he taught in ways that were effective and transformational for each. A related, hermeneutic function of the skillful means doctrine has been to help sacralize and legitimate Mahāyāna Buddhist sūtras – *scriptures* attributed to Śākyamuni Buddha that were actually composed by Buddhist sages centuries after he lived. Mahāyāna sūtras express diverse Buddhist doctrines, cosmologies and practices that emerged in a variety of Asian cultural contexts in the early centuries CE. Mahāyāna Buddhist scholars in India, East Asia and Tibet sought to make systematic sense of competing messages in these Buddhist scriptures, and in earlier Buddhist scriptures, not by historicizing them, but by attributing them all to the Buddha's skillful way of teaching the Dharma in different phases of his own teaching career during his lifetime in ancient India.[5]

Donald Lopez, in his essay, "On the Interpretation of the Mahāyāna Sūtras," explains how one such renowned Buddhist scholar, the seventh century Indian teacher Candrakīrti, employed the doctrine of skillful means as an interpretive principle to gain control over all previous Buddhist scriptures and traditions by depicting them as preparatory steps taught by Śākyamuni Buddha toward the realization of Candrakīrti's own Mahāyāna perspective. In other words, Lopez explained, Candrakīrti naively identified his own seventh century CE Mahāyāna

---

4 Jay Garfield, "Buddhism and Modernity," in *The Buddhist World* ed. John Powers (New York: Routledge, 2016), 303–4.

5 Ronald Davidson, "An Introduction to the Standards of Scriptural Authenticity in Indian Buddhism," in *Chinese Buddhist Apocrypha*, ed. Robert Buswell (Honolulu: Univ. of Hawaii Press, 1990), 291–323; John Makransky, "Historical Consciousness as an Offering to the Trans-historical Buddha," in *Buddhist Theology*, ed. Roger Jackson and John Makransky (New York: Routledge, 2000), 111–35; David McMahan, *Empty Vision: Metaphor and Visionary Imagery in Mahāyāna Buddhism* (London: RoutledgeCurzon, 2002), 99–110; Peter N. Gregory, *Tsung-mi and the Sinification of Buddhism* (Honolulu: Univ. of Hawaii Press, 2002), 93–114.

perspective on the Buddhist scriptures with Śākyamuni Buddha's fifth century BCE point of view on them.[6]

What are Lopez's conclusions? Taking Candrakīrti as his example, Lopez asserts that the Mahāyāna Buddhist commentator's basic goal in explaining a scripture's meaning is to pretend that he can replicate the Buddha's intention behind the scripture. Such an interpretive approach, wrote Lopez, is, in Hans Georg Gadamer's terms, "romantic" and "inadequate," because the Buddhist commentator is unaware both of the historical nature of the text he comments on and of his own historically conditioned perspective on it. The goal of the Buddhist interpreter then, Lopez declares, is to use the doctrine of skillful means to reinterpret diverse Buddhist literary and philosophical traditions in a homogenous way that supports the interpreter's own perspective on them all as the final perspective, within a closed system, while hiding the conditioned nature and newness of his project by ascribing his own perspective to the Buddha. In the end, Lopez concludes, Buddhist interpretation is the Buddhist exegete's projection of prejudice upon a received text.[7]

3.1.1 An Example of BCR's First Goal: Using Historical-Cultural Analysis to Inform New Buddhist Possibilities

As a PhD student who was a practicing Buddhist, I found Lopez's conclusions both insightful and partly disappointing. The problem for me was not his critical analysis, but *the ultimate purpose for doing it.* In his article, Lopez worked etically, as an '*outsider*' to Buddhist tradition – critiquing the hegemonic approach of Asian Buddhist commentators. Lopez, as a religious studies scholar who withholds judgment on normative questions, did not think to explore the normative implications of his findings for current Buddhist understanding. As an academic scholar, I appreciated his critical findings. But as someone who also practices within Buddhist communities East and West, I saw his conclusions as merely preliminary to important questions that he never raised. How might these historical findings inform current Buddhist traditions, which still draw heavily on commentators like Candrakīrti in their understanding of Buddhist texts? Could Lopez's critical findings contribute something *positive* to Buddhist traditions today – strengthening their ability to meet the historical consciousness of the modern

6 Donald Lopez, "On the Interpretation of the Mahāyāna Sūtras" in *Buddhist Hermeneutics,* ed. Donald Lopez (Honolulu: Univ. of Hawaii Press, 1988), 47–70.
7 Donald Lopez, "On the Interpretation of the Mahāyāna Sūtras", 65–7.

world by updating their understanding of the historical nature of their texts and institutions? Lopez's essay provided an insightful hermeneutic of suspicion. What it lacked was a hermeneutic of retrieval: fresh normative reflection in light of his critical findings.[8]

I'll suggest one possible direction for such a hermeneutic of retrieval. As Lopez noted, Buddhist scholars like Candrakīrti used the doctrine of *skillful means* to project their own perspectives back onto the Buddha. But why did they do so? One reason is that that doctrine served, within the non-historicizing norms of Asian Buddhist cultures, to grant the legitimacy needed for fresh historical developments to take expression in new cultural syntheses, by attributing them to the Buddha himself. Candrakīrti drew on the hermeneutic norms available to him in his time, including the doctrine of the Buddha's skillful means, to help legitimize the fresh constructive synthesis of his thought – which related themes from Indian sūtras that post-date Śākyamuni with Madhyamaka and Yogācāra views of soteriology, ethics, contemplative theory, and Buddhahood/enlightenment. By equating his seventh century way of ordering such teachings with the skillful means of the Buddha from twelve hundred years earlier, Candrakīrti also valorized his system of thought, so it could be taken seriously within scholarly communities of Indian Buddhism in his time, as worthy of serious attention, critical reflection, and debate.

Like Candrakīrti in seventh century India, traditional Buddhist scholars in East Asian and Tibetan cultures have repeatedly drawn on the doctrine of skillful means to support fresh syntheses of Buddhist concepts with indigenous religious perspectives and cultural concerns, helping to legitimize diverse Buddhist traditions by anchoring each culturally conditioned system in scriptures associated with an unconditioned origin: the enlightened mind of Śakyamuni Buddha. So, for example, Tsung mi's 8th century construction of Hua yen Buddhism in China integrated Confucian moral principles and Daoist cosmogonies with a system of Buddhist teachings derived from Mahāyāna sūtras ascribed to Śākyamuni.[9] The origins of Chinese Ch'an (Zen) Buddhism were ascribed to lineages of transmission directly from Śākyamuni through Bodhidharma, partly hiding the historical nature of Ch'an as an eighth century Chinese synthesis of Mahāyāna Buddhist teachings with ontological and ethical concepts from Daoism and Mencian Confu-

8 See Vesna Wallace, "The Methodological Relevance of Contemporary Biblical Scholarship to the Study of Buddhism," in *Buddhist Theology: Critical Reflections by Contemporary Buddhist Scholars*, ed. Roger Jackson and John Makransky (New York: Routledge, 2000), 78–91, for ways that current biblical scholarship models the need to balance the hermeneutics of suspicion with the hermeneutics of retrieval in Buddhist studies.

9 Gregory, *Tsung-mi and the Sinification of Buddhism*, 255–94.

cianism.[10] Indigenous orientations toward faith and devotion among Chinese masses took shape within Pure Land Buddhist teachings from sutras composed by Indian and Chinese sages, generating Sinitic Buddhist devotional movements that were also legitimated, in part, by the attribution of those sūtras to Śākyamuni Buddha himself.[11] In Tibet, Mahāyāna and Vajrayāna Buddhist systems integrated indigenous Tibetan concerns and perspectives with teachings from Indian and Tibetan composed sutras and tantras that were also partly legitimated by their ascription to Śākyamuni and cosmic Buddhas and tantric deities associated with him.[12]

How, then, should Buddhists today read Mahāyāna scriptures and associated Asian Buddhist systems of thought and practice in light of this historical knowledge? Instead of viewing them anachronistically as teachings by Śākyamuni during different phases of his lifetime, we can understand them to represent a variety of Buddhist perspectives in conversation with each other and indigenous worldviews within diverse cultures over history. Mahāyāna scriptures and systems of thought in Asia thus comprise a record of cultural adaptations of the Dharma that Buddhists today can draw on to inform the current adaptations needed to meet current cultures. New critical Buddhist reflection is also now needed to consider what traditional Buddhist criteria should be drawn upon today to establish the legitimacy of developments in Buddhist thought and practice over history, other than anachronistic projection of them back to Śākyamuni – such as their effectiveness in eradicating mental roots of suffering and in supporting realization of the four noble truths, transcendental wisdom, universal compassion and associated qualities of enlightenment within diverse worldviews. In sum, the hermeneutic of retrieval I am suggesting uses Lopez's critical deconstruction of Candrakīrti's *closed* system of thought, which he had anachronistically ascribed to Śākyamuni, as a basis for now engaging diverse, culturally contextual sources of Dharmic revelation, which can be drawn upon to inform multiple, *unclosed* systems of Buddhist thought and practice in present and future contexts.

---

10 Thomas Kasulis, *Zen Action, Zen Person* (Honolulu: University of Hawaii Press, 1981), 16–38.
11 Arthur F. Wright, *Studies in Chinese Buddhism* (New Haven, CT: Yale University Press, 1990), 25–6.
12 Geoffrey Samuel, *Civilized Shamans: Buddhism in Tibetan Societies* (Washington: Smithsonian, 1993), 388–481; Robert Mayer, "History as a Challenge to Buddhism and Bon," in *History as a Challenge to Buddhism and Christianity* ed. Elizabeth Harris and John O'Grady (Ottilien: EOS, 2016), 169–90; David Snellgrove, *Indo-Tibetan Buddhism: Indian Buddhists and their Tibetan Successors* (Boston: Shambhala, 1987), 117–121.

Because this suggestion follows from historicizing what has not been previously historicized in Asian Buddhist cultures, it is a relatively new normative proposal for traditional Buddhist institutions. If taken seriously, it would generate a strong new Buddhist interest in lots of new *intra*-Buddhist learning – since each Buddhist tradition models for each other tradition brilliant ways of adapting Buddhist teachings to new cultural contexts that make Buddhist paths of liberation freshly practicable. Each Buddhist tradition could be newly seen in that light as a precious resource for fresh doctrinal and practice reflection for each other Buddhist tradition. Since Buddhist traditions are also products of repeated integration of non-Buddhist religious, cultural and cosmological elements into new Buddhist frameworks (as previously noted with regard to China and Tibet), this historicized view of Buddhism should also motivate strong Buddhist interest in *inter*-religious and inter-disciplinary dialogue – to become familiar with non-Buddhist patterns of thought and practice in current cultures that, as in the past, must inform whatever new forms Buddhism will take today and in the future. I am making these normative suggestions for Buddhist traditions from an academic, critical-constructive Buddhist perspective. These suggestions seem to accord with a stance taken by Luis Gomez, a leading scholar of Buddhism, who wrote that Buddhist studies scholars render a service both to Buddhists, and to the role of criticism in the academy, by helping to preserve alternative voices both within Buddhism and within the academy.[13]

3.1.2 Other Examples of BCR's First Goal: Drawing on Feminist Analysis, Socioeconomic Analysis, and Cognitive Science to Inform New Buddhist Possibilities

What has been said so far provides one extended example of the first goal of Buddhist critical-constructive reflection (BCR) – to draw on academic disciplines, in this case historical analysis, together with emic/insider Buddhist understandings, to inform Buddhism in fresh, normative ways. Another prominent example of this first goal of BCR is Buddhist feminist analysis, which employs historical and social analysis to clear the way for a hermeneutic of retrieval that raises up key Buddhist principles upon which to build non-patriarchal Buddhist institutions and systems of practice – by supporting women teachers, restoring full monastic ordination for women who seek it, and promoting economic alternatives for

13 Luis Gomez, "Unspoken Paradigms: Meanderings through the Metaphors of a Field," *Journal of the International Association of Buddhist Studies* 18, no. 2 (1995), 216.

young women in society. Leaders in such feminist critical-constructive work have included Chatsurman Kabilsingh (Dhammananda Bhikkuní), Ouyporn Khuankaew, Rita Gross, Karma Lekshe Tsomo, Anne Klein, Hsiao Lan Hu and others.[14]

Another important example of the first goal of BCR is illustrated by the work of figures such as Sulak Sivaraksa, Thich Nhat Hanh, A. T. Ariyaratne, Bhikku Bodhi and David Loy. These Buddhist teachers have used modern social and economic analysis to reframe the Buddhist four noble truths, moral precepts, divine abodes, and concepts of liberation as both spiritual and socio-political principles for diagnosing and addressing sufferings connected with modern dehumanizing socioeconomic forces. Their ways of combining etic social analysis with emic Buddhist principles to integrate personal and social liberative praxis has reframed Buddhism for their followers in normative ways, while also bringing them into dialogue with current social theorists and with Christian theologians.[15] Another example of the first goal of BCR involves drawing on areas of cognitive science to help modern Buddhist students who are educated in science and want to engage in traditional practices do so in a more fully embodied way, e.g. by relating the sensory, affective, cognitive, and motor aspects of Buddhist ritual-devotional practices to current theories of embodied and grounded cognition.[16]

14 See Karma Lekshe Tsomo, ed. *Buddhist Women and Social Justice: Ideals, Challenges and Achievements.* (Albany, NY: State University of New York Press, 2004); Rita Gross, *Buddhism after Patriarchy: A Feminist History, Analysis, and Reconstruction of Buddhism.* (Albany, NY: State University of New York Press, 1993); Hsiao-Lan Hu, *This-Worldly Nibbana: A Buddhist Feminist Social Ethic for Peacemaking in the Global Community.* (Albany: State University of New York, 2011); Lori Meeks, "Feminist Approaches to the Study of Buddhism," in *Oxford Bibliographies Online: Buddhism*, ed. Richard Payne, accessed October 7, 2020, https://www.oxfordbibliographies.com/display/document/obo-9780195393521/obo-9780195393521-0060.xml?rskey=9yJMyE&result=102.

15 See Sallie B. King, *Socially Engaged Buddhism* (Honolulu: University of Hawaii Press, 2009), 13–66, 96–136; Sulak Sivaraksa, *The Wisdom of Sustainability: Buddhist Economics for the 21st Century* (London: Souvenir Press, 2009); Bhikku Bodhi, *Facing the Future: Four Essays* (Kandy, Sri Lanka: Buddhist Publication Society, 2009), 1–54; David Loy, *The Great Awakening: A Buddhist Social Theory* (Somerville, MA: Wisdom Publications, 2003), 1–52.

16 Paul Condon and John Makransky. "Recovering the Relational Starting Point of Compassion Training," *Perspectives on Psychological Science* 15, no. 6 (August 2020), 1346–62, accessed June 10, 2024, https://doi.org/10.31231/osf.io/dmxj7; Paul Condon and John Makransky, "Sustainable Compassion Training: Integrating Meditation Theory with Psychological Science," *Frontiers in Psychology* 11, (September 2020), accessed June 10, 2024, https://www.frontiersin.org/journals/psychology/articles/10.3389/fpsyg.2020.02249/full.

3.2 The Second Goal of BCR in Buddhist Asia and the West: Drawing on Buddhism to Expand Knowledge and Address Culturally Contextualized Needs

While the first goal of BCR is to draw on current areas of knowledge to inform aspects of Buddhism, the second goal of BCR is to draw on aspects of Buddhism to inform current areas of knowledge and to address current needs. This second kind of goal has also played an important part in the history of Buddhism in Asia. Buddhist teachers and communities have drawn on a wide variety of Buddhist disciplines – ritual, meditative, philosophical, ethical, psychological, literary, and artistic – to meet many culturally situated needs and concerns in Asia. These have included the need for physical and mental healing; for help in dying and rebirth; for promoting harmonious relationships with ancestors, indigenous deities, and rival clans; for averting natural disasters; for creating new ethical and cosmological frameworks for societies, and for generating new kinds of learning in literature, philosophy, medicine, the arts, and more. The history of Asian Buddhism is thus, in part, the history of the second goal of BCR – drawing on Buddhist resources to meet numerous cultural needs and to introduce many new forms of knowledge.[17] In East Asian and Tibetan cultures, to address so many mundane needs and concerns was not seen as contradicting the supramundane Buddhist concern to realize nirvāṇa and enlightenment, since mundane and supramundane applications of Buddhist power were *both* viewed as essential aspects of Buddhist participation in society. Mundane applications function as skillful means to enact Buddhist compassion in concrete ways, while garnering the social support needed for Buddhist institutions to preserve the full range of Bud-

17 On practical applications of Asian Buddhist ethical frameworks and ritual and meditative powers to meet diverse culturally situated human needs, see e.g. Arthur F. Wright, *Studies in Chinese Buddhism* (New Haven, CT: Yale University, 1990), 1–33; Stephan Beyer, *The Cult of Tara: Magic and Ritual in Tibet* (Los Angeles, CA: Univ. of California Press, 1978), 227–360; Geoffrey Samuel, *Civilized Shamans: Buddhism in Tibetan Societies* (Washington D.C.: Smithsonian Institution Press, 1993), 176–98, 258–69, 309–35. Excellent resources for this are: Donald S. Lopez, ed., *Buddhism in Practice* (Princeton: Princeton University Press,1995); Donald S. Lopez, ed., *Religions of Tibet in Practice* (Princeton: Princeton University Press, 1997); Donald S. Lopez, ed., *Religions of India in Practice* (Princeton: Princeton University Press, 1995); Donald S. Lopez, ed., *Religions of China in Practice* (Princeton: Princeton University Press, 1996); George Tanabe, *Religions of Japan in Practice*, (Princeton: Princeton University Press, 1999); Robert Buswell, *Religions of Korea in Practice* (Princeton: Princeton University Press, 2007); David Gorden White, ed., *Tantra in Practice* (Princeton: Princeton University Press, 2000).

dhist learning, both for attaining enlightenment and for addressing mundane needs.[18]

This repeated historical synthesis of Buddhism with indigenous cultures that I've been summarizing continues today. In modern Asian and Western forms of Buddhism, this synthesis prominently includes elements of Western modernity. In current Asian cultures, Buddhist concepts are integrated with modern social, economic and political theories as resources for Buddhist thinkers to suggest alternatives to neoliberal capitalism and autocratic communist systems. In response to national traumas, poverty, and violence in Southeast Asia, Tibet, and China, a number of Asian Buddhist leaders, such as Thich Nhat Hanh, Sulak Sivaraksa, Buddhadasa, the Dalai Lama, A.T. Ariyaratne, Chatsurman Kabilsingh, and others have promoted modern kinds of social reform, human rights, and progressive cultural, political and environmental practices informed by Buddhist principles.[19]

Westerners who have taken a strong interest in Buddhism, or converted to it, grew up within a modern worldview that is largely based in Western philosophical and religious assumptions, including scientific rationalism, romantic and transcendentalist notions of spirituality, the prominence of psychotherapy, individualism, egalitarianism, democracy, and modern Christian concepts of social justice and service. Conditioned by that worldview, many Western Buddhists have brought into their interpretations of Buddhism their own prior commitments to progressive so-

---

18 On skillful means (upāya kauśalya) as a doctrine that helps bridge the pragmatic mundane goals and the supramundane enlightenment goals of Buddhist cultures, see Geoffrey Samuel, *Civilized Shamans: Buddhism in Tibetan Societies* (Washington D.C.: Smithsonian Institution Press, 1993), 269. For historical overviews of ways that Buddhist teachings and practices adapted to meet the worldviews, needs and concerns of Chinese, Japanese and Tibetan cultures, see, e.g.: Geoffrey Samuel, *Civilized Shamans*, 436–573; Wright, *Studies in Chinese Buddhism*; Peter N. Gregory, ed., *Traditions of Meditation in Chinese Buddhism* (Honolulu: University of Hawaii Press, 1986); Kenneth Ch'en, *Buddhism in China: A Historical Survey* (Princeton: Princeton University Press, 1964); E. Zurcher, *The Buddhist Conquest of China: The Spread and Adaptation of Buddhism in Early Medieval China* (Leiden: Brill, 1972); Daigan Matsunaga and Alicia Matsunaga, *Foundation of Japanese Buddhism* (Tokyo: Eikyōji, 1974); Joseph M. Kitagawa, *Religion in Japanese History* (New York: Columbia University Press, 1990).

19 Sallie B. King, "Socially Engaged Buddhism," in *Buddhism in the Modern World*, ed. David McMahan (New York: Routledge, 2012), 195–214; Sallie B. King, *Socially Engaged Buddhism* (Honolulu: University of Hawaii Press, 2009), 67–158; Dalai Lama, *Ethics for the New Millennium* (New York: Riverhead Books, 1999), 161–218; Christopher Queen and Sallie B. King, eds., *Engaged Buddhism: Buddhist Liberation Movements in Asia* (Albany, NY: State University of New York Press), 121–236, 259–364.

cial, political and ecological ideals, personal spirituality, and therapeutic self-improvement.[20]

4 The Second Goal of BCR within the Current Synthesis of Buddhism with Modernity

This synthesis of Buddhism with modernity East and West has conditioned the forms that the second goal of BCR has taken in academia and in Buddhist movements that apply Buddhism to contemporary concerns. Buddhist thought and practice is drawn on to inform areas of philosophy, psychology, social theory, business practices, economics, education, governance, ecology, race theory, and more. Buddhist meditation methods, adapted into secularized forms, are applied to help treat physical and mental illnesses, addiction and trauma, and to inform new directions of research in clinical psychology, cognitive science, neuroscience, and medicine. Buddhist contemplative practices are also adapted to help healthcare professionals, therapists, social workers, educators and activists avoid compassion fatigue and become more resilient and responsive to those they serve. Socially engaged Buddhist movements in Asia and the West have integrated Buddhist principles with social, economic, and political analyses to critique global consumerism, to offer new perspectives on human rights, environmental ethics, economics, criminal justice, and to address social problems like poverty and homelessness, both by meeting needs and by working for systemic changes. These applications of Buddhism to modern problems bridge Buddhist and secular worlds of discourse, and also bridge academic and non-academic worlds of analysis, service and activism.[21]

---

20 David McMahan, *The Making of Buddhist Modernism* (New York: Oxford University Press, 2008), 3–25, 241–54; Jay Garfield, "Buddhism and Modernity," in *The Buddhist World*, ed. John Powers (New York, Routledge: 2016), 299–303; Bhikku Bodhi, "Manifesting the Buddha Dharma in a Secular Age," in *Secularizing Buddhism: New Perspectives on a Dynamic Tradition*, ed. Richard Payne (Boulder, CO: Shambhala, 2021), 164–9; Amod Lele, "Disengaged Buddhism," *Journal of Buddhist Ethics* 26 (2019): 268–78; Shodhin Geiman, *Alone in a World of Wounds* (Eugene, OR: Cascade Books, 2022), 2–5, 74, 90–2, 183–95, 204–8.

21 Jay Garfield, *Engaging Buddhism: Why it Matters to Philosophy* (New York: Oxford University Press, 2015); Susan Darlington, "Contemporary Buddhism and Ecology," in *Oxford Handbook of Contemporary Buddhism*, ed. Michael Jerryson (New York: Oxford University Press, 2016), 487–503; Stephanie Kaza, *Green Buddhism: Practice and Compassionate Action in Uncertain Times* (Boulder, CO: Shambhala, 2019); John Stanley, David Loy, and Gyurme Dorje, eds., *A Buddhist Response to the Climate Emergency* (Somerville, MA: Wisdom, 2009); Edwin Ng, "Towards a Dialogue between Buddhist Social Theory and Affect Studies on the Ethico-Political Significance of Mindfulness," *Journal*

4.1 Buddhist Accommodation to Modern Frameworks: Positive Contributions and Problematics

4.1.1 Socially Engaged Buddhism as Example: Positive Contributions

Thus, as David McMahan has noted, Buddhism is often now formulated by Buddhists and others in the languages of Western modernity, the languages of Western psychology, social science, ethics, and so forth. With McMahan, I want to raise up two implications of this reformulation of Buddhism into languages of modernity. *First*, as in past cultural adaptations of Buddhism, Buddhism's current adaptations to modern cultures enable it to offer people new perspectives, insights and critiques in their own languages and within their own worldviews. *Secondly*, as Buddhism makes new contributions in those ways, it also risks accommodating itself so much to modern assumptions and values, that it may lose part of its ability to critique them or to offer important alternatives to them.[22]

Let's look briefly at those two points, with modern Socially engaged Buddhism (SEB) as an example. 1) How is SEB making significant new contributions? 2) How does it also risk accommodating itself too much to modernity?

---

of Buddhist Ethics 21 (2014): 353–84; Tania Singer and Mathieu Ricard, eds., *Caring Economics* (New York: Picador, 2015); Trine Brox and Elizabeth Williams Oerberg, "Buddhism, Business and Economics," in ed. Michael Jerryson, *Oxford Handbook of Contemporary Buddhism* (New York: Oxford University Press, 2016), 504–17; Bhikku Bodhi, *Facing the Future: Four Essays*, 1–54; Sallie B. King, *Socially Engaged Buddhism*; Pamela Ayo Yetunde and Cheryl Giles. *Black & Buddhist: What Buddhism can Teach us about Race, Resilience, Transformation & Freedom* (Boulder: Shambhala, 2020); Hugh Nicholson, *Buddhism, Cognitive Science and the Doctrine of Selflessness* (New York: Routledge, 2023); Francisco Varela,, *Ethical Know-How: Action, Wisdom, and Cognition.* (Stanford, CA: Stanford University Press, 1992); Francisco Varela, Evan Thompson and Eleanor Rosch, *The Embodied Mind: Cognitive Science and Human Experience* (Cambridge, MA: MIT Press, 1993); Ronald Purser, David Forbes, and Adam Burke, eds. *Handbook of Mindfulness: Culture, Context, and Social Engagement.* (Switzerland: Springer, 2016); Emma Seppälä et al., *Oxford Handbook of Compassion Science* (New York: Oxford University Press, 2017); Paul Gilbert, ed., *Compassion: Concepts, Research and Applications* (New York: Routledge, 2017); Christopher Germer and Ronald Siegel, eds., *Wisdom and Compassion in Psychotherapy: Deepening mindfulness in clinical practice* (New York: Guilford Press, 2012), 203–92; J. Mark Williams and Jon Kabat-Zinn, "Mindfulness: Diverse Perspectives on its Meaning, Origins, and Multiple Applications at the Intersection of Science and Dharma," *Contemporary Buddhism* 12, no. 1 (June 2011): 1–18; William S. Waldron, "Buddhism in Psychology and Psychotherapy," in *Oxford Bibliographies: Buddhism* (New York: Oxford University Press, 2021), accessed June 10, 2024, https://www.oxfordbibliographies.com/display/document/obo-9780195393521/obo-9780195393521-0130.xml; "Insights: Journey into the Heart of Contemplative Science," Mind and Life Institute, accessed June 10, 2024, https://www.mindandlife.org/insights/.

22 David McMahan, *The Making of Buddhist Modernism*, 260.

One valuable contribution of socially engaged Buddhism, I think, is the distinctive link it makes between individual and social conditioning in diagnosing and addressing social problems. Classical Buddhism identifies kleśa – delusive tendencies of misperception (avidyā), greed (rāga), and ill-will (dveṣa) – as primary causes of individual suffering, because they drive our minds to seek stable well-being by clinging to insubstantial phenomena, which generates dysfunctional reactions to our world, which further strengthens those delusive tendencies in our minds. Drawing from the social sciences, Socially engaged Buddhist leaders link that classical focus on inner, individual causes of suffering with outer, social causes of suffering, by arguing that these internal delusive tendencies take shape externally in destructive forms of social, economic and political organization, which further strengthen the delusive tendencies in the minds of all the individuals involved. Because individual and social conditioning thus feed on each other, they argue, we cannot effectively address either individual suffering or the social, political and ecological crises of our time without addressing both types of conditioning – individual and social.[23]

If, as in most modern social activism, we work only to change social and economic systems, the individual conditioning of delusion, greed and ill-will in everyone involved keeps reasserting itself in ways that distort and corrupt any new social system. But if we focus, as in classical Buddhism, just on practices to transform individuals, the conditioning influence of social structures continues to instill and strengthen the delusive tendencies in individuals. So, to undercut these delusive tendencies, Socially engaged Buddhism offers culturally adaptive practices from diverse Buddhist traditions that must be applied both individually and socially. In individual practice, cultivation of insight into interdependence and emptiness, together with unconditional compassion, becomes a force for individual awakening that applies its power socially to confront problems of inequality, poverty, militarism, and ecological destruction. And in their social analysis and practice, engaged Buddhists draw both on Buddhist principles and on the social sciences, to critique neoliberal economic systems that promote an endless expansion of greed for products and to suggest ways to reorganize economies around a

23 Bodhi, *Facing*, 5–42; Donald Swearer, "Sulak Sivaraksa's Buddhist Vision for Renewing Society" in *Engaged Buddhism: Buddhist Liberation Movements in Asia*, ed. Christopher Queen and Sallie B. King (Albany, NY: State University of New York, 1996), 216–23; George Bond, "A.T. Ariyaratne and the Sarvodaya Sharmadana Movement in Sri Lanka," in *Engaged Buddhism: Buddhist Liberation Movements in Asia*, ed. Christopher Queen and Sallie B. King, 124–31; David Loy, *The Great Awakening: A Buddhist Social Theory*, 22–3, 35–6, 87, 187–97; Ken Jones, *The Social Face of Buddhism: An Approach to Political and Social Activism* (Boston: Wisdom Publications, 1989), 193–200.

broader range of actual needs: material, ethical, cultural, ecological, and spiritual.[24] SEB thus offers not only a theoretical analysis of the interdependence of personal and social dimensions of suffering and liberation, but also concrete instruction for how to engage that interdependence in practice as a transformative power for both dimensions together – personal and social. I do think that makes an important contribution to the modern world.

4.1.2 Socially Engaged Buddhism as Example: Problematics

But, as noted, as Buddhist movements like SEB offer such contributions to modern societies, they also risk accommodating themselves so much to modern assumptions that they can lose their ability to challenge those assumptions, or to offer significant alternatives to them. In what follows I will speak to this point as an engaged Buddhist constructive thinker who practices in the Mahāyāna and Vajrayāna Buddhist traditions.

While the most prominent Asian Buddhist leaders of SEB (such as Thich Nhat Hanh, the Dalai Lama, Venerable Chengyen, Sulak Sivaraksa, A.T. Ariyaratne, Mahāghosananda, Chatsurman Kabilsingh) are renowned for embodying awakened qualities that inform their social practices from long training in established Buddhist cultures and institutions of Asia, this is not the case for many Western socially engaged Buddhists, who grew up in a cultural world of modern assumptions that contradict key Buddhist teachings. What modern assumptions? These include the common modern assumption that temporal well-being in the context of one lifetime is the ultimate human value (not nirvana or enlightenment); the common assumption that physical and social conditions are the only real causes of suffering (not the delusive mental tendencies that Buddhism identifies); and the common assumption that obvious forms of suffering are the only kind that exist or the only kind worth addressing (ignoring subliminal levels of suffering taught in Buddhism that drive harmful individual and social behaviors).[25] Those modern assumptions

---

24 See note 23 for references. See also Sallie B. King, *Socially Engaged Buddhism*, 99–113, and the description of Bhutan's Gross National Happiness Index on the website of the Oxford Poverty and Human Development Initiative, "Gross National Happiness," Oxford Poverty and Human Development Initiative, accessed June 10, 2024, https://ophi.org.uk/policy/bhutan-gnh-index/#:~:text=According%20to%20the%202022%20GNH,2010%20to%2048.1%25%20in%202022.

25 Such modernistic, pre-conscious assumptions are shared by many Westerners involved in modern emancipatory movements, including Christian liberation theology and socially engaged Buddhism. Several such assumptions were critiqued in John Makransky, "How Buddhist and Christian Epistemologies Should Inform and Correct Each Other," *Buddhist Christian Studies Jour-*

are part of the preunderstanding of many Westerners involved in progressive movements, including socially engaged Buddhism. Those assumptions support the tendency in modern emancipatory movements to give all one's attention to establishing conditions for people's temporal well-being. But for engaged Buddhists, that exclusive focus on working to change the world's conditions can eclipse levels of Buddhist practice that focus on the empty, unconditioned nature of the world, where the unconditioned well-being and freedom of enlightenment is said to be found, which is associated with all-inclusive compassion and liberating activity that is directed, equally, to all beings caught in the sufferings of conditioned life, death and rebirth.

Even when Western engaged Buddhists (like me) echo their Asian teachers in asserting the simultaneous practice of personal and social liberation, we are not necessarily operating at that level of practice. We can wind up implicitly reversing the primary and secondary goals of Buddhism: taking the secondary social concern for people's *conditioned* freedom and well-being as primary, while downplaying the primary Buddhist goal of realizing *unconditioned* freedom and well-being, enlightenment, as a foundational support for all else.[26] One sign of that reversal of priorities is the pervasive habit among modern activists of cultivating an affective preference for the so-called 'oppressed' over the 'oppressors,' to value one group as worthy while devaluing and implicitly despising the other group, which contradicts the literally unconditional and all-inclusive kind of compassion cultivated in Buddhist traditions. The latter is a compassion that recognizes an equal depth of dignity and worth in all beings, within their buddha nature. And it is a compassion that focuses not just on obvious sufferings, but also on less conscious levels of suffering and conditioning in everyone, which drive our harmful personal and social behaviors.

I am not arguing for reducing the focus of modern Buddhist activity just to ultimate, supramundane Buddhist goals. As I noted earlier, the history of Buddhism has always included a secondary focus on responding to temporal needs. I am arguing against losing the *primary* Buddhist goal of unconditioned liberation and well-being in our attachment to *secondary* goals of conditioned liberation and well-being – social and personal.[27] I have observed in myself and other Buddhists involved in service and activism, a tendency, conditioned by our modern

nal 39 (2019): 241–58. On such modernistic assumptions, also see Bodhi, *Secularizing Buddhism*, 164–78.

26 Bodhi, *Secularizing*, 177–8; Bardwell Smith, as quoted in Queen, *Engaged Buddhism*, 17; Geiman, *Alone in a World of Wounds*, 2–16, 49–50, 113-–6. Ken Jones, "Liberation is Indivisible: The Convergence of Buddhism and Modernity," unpublished manuscript, 190–5.

27 See references in note 26. Also see Lele, "Disengaged Buddhism," 281–3.

upbringings, to absolutize the relative truth of the conditioned world in a way that loses awareness of the ultimate truth of it, the empty unconditioned nature of that world. In Buddhist understanding, it is the awareness of ultimate truth, emptiness, that liberates the mind from habitual identification with its reified perceptions, thoughts and reactions, and thereby frees the mind for greater discernment, equanimity, perseverance, creative responsiveness, and unbiased compassion for action. These powers of awakening are what help the mind avoid replicating its delusive tendencies, the inner causes of suffering, while working to address social suffering.[28] That is why cultivating the insight of emptiness with such awakening power is central to the bodhisattva path. If the primary Buddhist goal of inmost liberation does not remain primary in socially engaged Buddhism, delusive inner causes of suffering will be subliminally reinforced in the heat of service and activism, and the secondary Buddhist goal of promoting temporal well-being can not be actualized as effectively. Thus, Buddhism's fuller contribution to the modern world will be severely limited.

To help avoid that, I suggest the need for renewed emphasis in SEB on participation in, and support for, Buddhist institutions of intensive study and practice, including monastic institutions, as foundational for modern Buddhists to learn how to progress into deepening levels of practice that touch on the empty, unconditioned nature of all things while serving and working for change in the conditioned world.

5 Conclusion

In sum, the term Buddhist critical-constructive reflection (BCR, also called Buddhist theology) first emerged at the end of the twentieth century in reaction to the way knowledge was organized at that time in the academic study of religion. But analogues of the two goals of modern BCR can be seen throughout the history of Buddhism in Asia and the West. In each time and place, Buddhists have drawn on perspectives from the new culture to reframe Buddhism in ways that help it make fresh contributions to that culture and to thrive within it. The two goals of modern

28 Thich Nhat Hanh, *Love in Action: Writings on Nonviolent Social Change* (Berkeley, CA: Parallax Press, 1993), 65–72. Thich Nhat Hanh uses the term "interbeing" to signify awareness of the empty, interdependent nature of phenomena. Santikaro Bhikku, "Buddhadasa Bhikku: Life and Society through the Natural Eyes of Voidness," in *Engaged Buddhism: Buddhist Liberation Movements in Asia*, ed. Christopher Queen and Sallie B. King (Albany: State University of New York Press, 1996), 173.

BCR mirror those two aspects of Buddhist enculturation over history: Buddhism informing and affecting the new culture as it is also being informed and affected by it. This constitutes an historical-cultural way of understanding the doctrine of skillful means – the ability of the Dharma to integrate with cultures in ways that effectively meet diverse mentalities and make new things possible. But, as Buddhism makes new contributions in these ways to any culture past or present, it also risks succumbing so much to the dominant assumptions of that culture that it can lose some of its ability to offer important alternatives to them. Hence, there is always a Buddhist need for critical-constructive reflection, to keep newly learning from and contributing to current cultures, while also cultivating a healthy critical awareness of the dominant assumptions of those cultures.

John Makransky PhD, has been Associate Professor of Buddhism and Comparative Theology at Boston College, Senior Academic Advisor for Chökyi Nyima Rinpoche's Centre of Buddhist Studies at Rangjung Yeshe Institute in Nepal, president of the Society of Buddhist-Christian studies, Fellow of the Mind and Life Institute, and Senior Editor for the Buddhism section of the St. Andrews Encyclopedia of Theology. John was also one of the leaders of a scholarly movement in the American Academy of Religion to establish a unit dedicated to Buddhist Critical-Constructive Reflection ("Buddhist Theology"). John has published books and articles that focus on connections between devotion, compassion, and wisdom in Indian and Tibetan Buddhism, on adapting Buddhist practices to meet contemporary minds, and on theoretical issues in interfaith learning, including Buddhahood Embodied (1997), Buddhist Theology (co-edited with Roger Jackson, 2000), Awakening through Love (2007), and How Compassion Works (co-authored with Paul Condon, 2024). John has also developed the Sustainable Compassion Training model of contemplative practice (SCT) to help modern Buddhists, people of diverse faiths, and those in caring roles and professions generate a more sustaining and unconditional power of compassion and awareness to support their lives and work (https://sustainablecompassion.org).

Bibliography

Alles, Gregory. "Study of Religion: An Overview." In *Encyclopedia of Religion*, 2nd edition. Vol. 13. Edited by Lindsay Jones, 8761–7. Detroit: Macmillan Reference, 2005.

Beyer, Stephan. *The Cult of Tara: Magic and Ritual in Tibet*. Los Angeles, CA: Univ. of California Press, 1978.

Bhikku, Santikaro. "Buddhadasa Bhikku: Life and Society through the Natural Eyes of Voidness." In *Engaged Buddhism: Buddhist Liberation Movements in Asia*. Edited by Christopher Queen and Sallie B. King. Albany: State University of New York Press, 1996.

Bodhi, Bhikku. *Facing the Future: Four Essays*. Kandy, Sri Lanka: Buddhist Publication Society, 2009.

Bodhi, Bhikku. "Manifesting the Buddha Dharma in a Secular Age." In *Secularizing Buddhism: New Perspectives on a Dynamic Tradition*, edited by Richard Payne, 163–84. Boulder, CO: Shambhala, 2021, 164–9.

Bond, George. "A.T. Ariyaratne and the Sarvodaya Sharmadana Movement in Sri Lanka." In *Engaged Buddhism: Buddhist Liberation Movements in Asia*, edited by Christopher Queen and Sallie B. King, 124–31. Albany: State University of New York Press, 1996.

Brox, Trine and Elizabeth Williams Oerberg. "Buddhism, Business and Economics." In *Oxford Handbook of Contemporary Buddhism*, edited by Michael Jerryson, 504–17. New York: Oxford University Press, 2016.

Buswell, Robert. *Religions of Korea in Practice*. Princeton: Princeton University Press, 2007.

Cabezon, José. "The Discipline and its Other: The Dialectic of Alterity in the Study of Religion." *Journal of the American Academy of Religion* 74, no. 1 (March 2006): 21–38.

Ch'en, Kenneth. *Buddhism in China: A Historical Survey*. Princeton: Princeton University Press, 1964.

Condon, Paul, and John Makransky. "Recovering the Relational Starting Point of Compassion Training." *Perspectives on Psychological Science* 15, no. 6 (August 2020): 1346–62. Accessed June 10, 2024. https://doi.org/10.31231/osf.io/dmxj7.

Condon, Paul and John Makransky. "Sustainable Compassion Training: Integrating Meditation Theory with Psychological Science." *Frontiers in Psychology* 11, (September 2020). Accessed June 10, 2024. https://www.frontiersin.org/journals/psychology/articles/10.3389/fpsyg.2020.02249/full.

Dalai Lama. *Ethics for the New Millennium*. New York: Berkely Publishing, 1999.

Darlington, Susan. "Contemporary Buddhism and Ecology." In *Oxford Handbook of Contemporary Buddhism*, edited by Michael Jerryson, 487–503. New York: Oxford University Press, 2016.

Davidson, Ronald. "An Introduction to the Standards of Scriptural Authenticity in Indian Buddhism." In *Chinese Buddhist Apocrypha*. Edited by Robert Buswell, 291–323. Honolulu: Univ. of Hawaii Press, 1990.

Garfield, Jay. "Buddhism and Modernity." In *The Buddhist World*, edited by John Powers, 294–304. New York: Routledge, 2016.

Garfield, Jay. *Engaging Buddhism: Why it Matters to Philosophy*. New York: Oxford University Press, 2015.

Geiman, Shodhin. *Alone in a World of Wounds*. Eugene, OR: Cascade Books, 2022.

Germer, Christopher, and Ronald Siegel, eds. *Wisdom and Compassion in Psychotherapy: Deepening mindfulness in clinical practice*. New York: Guilford Press, 2012.

Gilbert, Paul, ed. *Compassion: Concepts, Research and Applications*. New York: Routledge, 2017.

Gomez, Luis. "Unspoken Paradigms: Meanderings through the Metaphors of a Field," *Journal of the International Association of Buddhist Studies* 18, no. 2 (1995): 183–230.

Gregory, Peter N., ed. *Traditions of Meditation in Chinese Buddhism*. Honolulu: University of Hawaii Press, 1986.

Gregory, Peter N. *Tsung-mi and the Sinification of Buddhism*. Honolulu: Univ. of Hawaii Press, 2002.

Gross, Rita. *Buddhism after Patriarchy: A Feminist History, Analysis, and Reconstruction of Buddhism*. Albany, NY: State University of New York Press, 1993.

Hu, Hsiao-Lan. *This-Worldly Nibbana: A Buddhist Feminist Social Ethic for Peacemaking in the Global Community*. Albany: State University of New York, 2011.

Jackson, Roger. "Buddhist Theology: Its Historical Context." In *Buddhist Theology: Critical Constructive Reflections by Contemporary Scholars*. Edited by Roger Jackson and John Makransky, 1–13. New York: Routledge, 2000.

Jackson, Roger and John Makransky, eds. *Buddhist Theology: Critical Reflections by Contemporary Buddhist Scholars*. Surrey, England: Curzon Press, 2000.

Jerryson, Michael, ed. *The Oxford Handbook of Contemporary Buddhism*. New York: Oxford University Press, 2017.

Jones, Ken. *The Social Face of Buddhism: An Approach to Political and Social Activism*. Boston: Wisdom Publications, 1989.
Jones, Ken. "Liberation is Indivisible: The Convergence of Buddhism and Modernity," unpublished manuscript.
Kasulis, Thomas. *Zen Action, Zen Person*. Honolulu: University of Hawaii Press, 1981.
Kaza, Stephanie. *Green Buddhism: Practice and Compassionate Action in Uncertain Times*. Boulder, CO: Shambhala, 2019.
King, Sallie B. *Socially Engaged Buddhism*. Honolulu: University of Hawaii Press, 2009.
King, Sallie B. "Socially Engaged Buddhism." In *Buddhism in the Modern World*. Edited by David McMahan, 195–214. New York: Routledge, 2012.
Kitagawa, Joseph M. *Religion in Japanese History*. New York: Columbia University Press, 1990.
Lele, Amod. "Disengaged Buddhism." *Journal of Buddhist Ethics* 26 (2019): 268–78.
Lopez, Donald S., ed. *Buddhism in Practice*. Princeton: Princeton University Press, 1995.
Lopez, Donald S. "On the Interpretation of the Mahāyāna Sūtras." In *Buddhist Hermeneutics*. Edited by Donald S. Lopez, 47–70. Honolulu: Univ. of Hawaii Press, 1988.
Lopez, Donald S., ed. *Religions of China in Practice*. Princeton: Princeton University Press, 1996.
Lopez, Donald S., ed. *Religions of India in Practice*. Princeton: Princeton University Press, 1995.
Lopez, Donald S., ed. *Religions of Tibet in Practice*. Princeton: Princeton University Press, 1997.
Loy, David. *The Great Awakening: A Buddhist Social Theory*. Sommerville, MA: Wisdom Publications, 2003.
Makransky, John. "Contemporary Academic Buddhist Theology: Its Emergence and Rationale." In *Buddhist Theology: Critical Constructive Reflections by Contemporary Scholars*. Edited by Roger Jackson and John Makransky, 14–21. New York: Routledge, 2000.
Makransky, John. "Historical Consciousness as an Offering to the Trans-historical Buddha." In *Buddhist Theology*. Edited by Roger Jackson and John Makransky, 111–35 (New York: Routledge, 2000).
Makransky, John. "How Buddhist and Christian Epistemologies Should Inform and Correct Each Other." *Buddhist Christian Studies Journal* 39 (2019): 241–58.
Matsunaga, Daigan, and Alicia Matsunaga. *Foundation of Japanese Buddhism*. Tokyo: Eikyōji, 1974.
Mayer, Robert. "History as a Challenge to Buddhism and Bon." In *History as a Challenge to Buddhism and Christianity*. Edited by Elizabeth Harris and John O'Grady, 169–90. Ottilien: EOS, 2016.
McMahan, David. *Empty Vision: Metaphor and Visionary Imagery in Mahāyāna Buddhism*. London: RoutledgeCurzon, 2002.
McMahan, David. *The Making of Buddhist Modernism*. New York: Oxford University Press, 2017.
Meeks, Lori. "Feminist Approaches to the Study of Buddhism." In *Oxford Bibliographies Online: Buddhism*. Edited by Richard Payne. Accessed October 7, 2020. https://www.oxfordbibliographies.com/display/document/obo-9780195393521/obo-9780195393521-0060.xml?rskey=9yJMyE&result=102.
Mind and Life Institute. "Insights: Journey into the Heart of Contemplative Science." Accessed June 10, 2024. https://www.mindandlife.org/insights/.
Nhat Hanh, Thich. *Love in Action: Writings on Nonviolent Social Change*. Berkeley, CA: Parallax Press, 1993.
Nicholson, Hugh. *Buddhism, Cognitive Science and the Doctrine of Selflessness*. New York: Routledge, 2023.
Ng, Edwin. "Towards a Dialogue between Buddhist Social Theory and Affect Studies on the Ethico-Political Significance of Mindfulness." *Journal of Buddhist Ethics* 21 (2014): 353–84.

Oxford Poverty and Human Development Initiative. "Gross National Happiness." Accessed June 10, 2024. https://ophi.org.uk/policy/bhutan-gnh-index/#:~:text=According%20to%20the%202022%20GNH,2010%20to%2048.1%25%20in%202022.

Purser, Ronald, David Forbes, and Adam Burke, eds. *Handbook of Mindfulness: Culture, Context, and Social Engagement.* Switzerland: Springer, 2016.

Queen, Christopher S., and Sallie B. King, eds. *Engaged Buddhism: Buddhist Liberation Movements in Asia.* Albany: State University of New York Press, 1996.

Samuel, Geoffrey. *Civilized Shamans: Buddhism in Tibetan Societies.* Washington D.C.: Smithsonian Institution Press, 1993.

Seppälä, Emma, Emiliana Simon-Thomas, Stephanie Brown, Monica Worline, C. Daryl Cameron, and James Doty, eds. *Oxford Handbook of Compassion Science.* New York: Oxford University Press, 2017.

Singer, Tania and Mathieu Ricard eds., *Caring Economics.* New York: Picador, 2015.

Sivaraksa, Sulak. *The Wisdom of Sustainability: Buddhist Economics for the 21st Century.* London: Souvenir Press, 2009.

Snellgrove, David. *Indo-Tibetan Buddhism: Indian Buddhists and their Tibetan Successors.* Boston: Shambhala, 1987.

Stanley, John, David Loy and Gyurme Dorje, eds. *A Buddhist Response to the Climate Emergency.* Sommerville, MA: Wisdom, 2009.

Swearer, Donald. "Sulak Sivaraksa's Buddhist Vision for Renewing Society." In *Engaged Buddhism: Buddhist Liberation Movements in Asia*, edited by Christopher Queen and Sallie King, 216–223. Albany, NY: State University of New York, 1996.

Tanabe, George, ed. *Religions of Japan in Practice.* Princeton: Princeton University Press, 1999.

Tsomo, Karma Lekshe, ed. *Buddhist Women and Social Justice: Ideals, Challenges and Achievements.* Albany, NY: State University of New York Press, 2004.

Varela, Francisco. *Ethical Know-How: Action, Wisdom, and Cognition.* Stanford, CA: Stanford University Press, 1992.

Varela, Francisco, Evan Thompson and Eleanor Rosch. *The Embodied Mind: Cognitive Science and Human Experience.* Cambridge, MA: MIT Press, 1993.

Waldron, William S. "Buddhism in Psychology and Psychotherapy." In *Oxford Bibliographies: Buddhism.* New York: Oxford University Press, 2021. Accessed June 10, 2024. https://www.oxfordbibliographies.com/display/document/obo-9780195393521/obo-9780195393521-0130.xml.

Wallace, Vesna. "The Methodological Relevance of Contemporary Biblical Scholarship to the Study of Buddhism." In *Buddhist Theology: Critical Reflections by Contemporary Buddhist Scholars.* Edited by Roger Jackson and John Makransky, 78–91. New York: Routledge, 2000.

White, David Gorden, ed. *Tantra in Practice.* Princeton: Princeton University Press, 2000.

Williams, J. Mark and Jon Kabat Zinn. "Mindfulness: Diverse Perspectives on its Meaning, Origins, and Multiple Applications at the Intersection of Science and Dharma." In *Contemporary Buddhism* 12, no. 1 (June 2011): 1–18.

Wright, Arthur F. *Studies in Chinese Buddhism.* New Haven, CT: Yale University, 1990.

Yancy, George and McRae, Emily, eds. *Buddhism and Whiteness: Critical Reflections.* Lanham, MD: Rowman & Littlefield, 2019.

Yetunde, Pamela Ayo and Cheryl Giles. *Black & Buddhist: What Buddhism can Teach us about Race, Resilience, Transformation & Freedom.* Boulder: Shambhala, 2020.

Zurcher, E. *The Buddhist Conquest of China: The Spread and Adaptation of Buddhism in Early Medieval China.* Leiden: Brill, 1972.

Lejla Demiri

An Islamic Approach to Islamic Studies? Muslim Faith Commitment in the European Orientalist Sphere

Our conference theme for this year is 'Religion from the Inside'. For some, this is an oxymoron: religion is, as in the Ghazalian tradition, a matter of 'tasting' (*dhawq*). On this view, the outsider can no more describe faith than a man can describe the taste of a dish which he has never tasted.[1] In Tübingen, Josef van Ess (1934–2021), despite his acknowledged position as the greatest interpreter of medieval Muslim theology, was able to insist that Muslims themselves possess the best understanding of the meaning of Muslim worship. As an outsider, he believed himself disadvantaged.[2]

But for others, insider spaces are caught in strong, poorly-understood currents and tides of personal need and loyalty, and hence can never provide the vantage point from which one can dispassionately observe, quantify, and conclude. In a way this argument supplies the crux of the Enlightenment project, so that departments of Theology and Religious Studies agonistically straddle the two worlds of the primitive and the rational, the subjective and the scientific, the tribal and the individual. In this zero-sum game, academe is seen as the theatre in which faith fights a slow retreating battle against a rival armed with more modern equipment. The outcome of this drama was always said to be obvious.

And yet this battlefield remains active, after at least two centuries of determined assaults, ambushes and inventive new strategies devised by each side. The field of honour has also been the site of *internal strife*, as neither secular modernity nor scriptural faith has found it possible to field a unified army. Anthropologists, philosophers, text critics, linguistic theorists and others cannot agree; but neither can the theologians or the religiously-sensitive students of the holy. Perhaps this is unsurprising, given the quite recent collapse of so many other progressist binaries. Modernity gives us blessings, but also challenges us with Black Swan threats such as climate change, Artificial Intelligence, genetics, and much else. Triumphalism of any kind has become difficult; a secularity or a religion

1 Al-Ghazālī, *The Ninety-Nine Beautiful Names of God*, trans. David B. Burrell and Nazih Daher (Cambridge: The Islamic Texts Society, 2004), 41–2.

2 As he expressed on various occasions at the Center for Islamic Theology in Tübingen. He was confident that Islamic theology will furnish an indispensable enrichment to the study of Islam in Germany.

https://doi.org/10.1515/9783111454658-003

that looks forward to a rational heaven on earth has been quite comprehensively chastened.

As someone who daily inhabits this arena, and in fact has located within it a peaceable but hopefully alert habitat, I propose today to describe a specific instance of this dialectic. I am someone who first learned Islam in a madrasa in the Balkans and then at the Imam-Hatip and Ilahiyat theology schools of secular Turkey; but I also studied at the Pontifical Gregorian University in Rome, and at Cambridge's Faculty of Divinity. I can claim to have visited and indeed somehow inhabited all these separate worlds. And in my present habitus in a German secular university, cradle of the nineteenth-century Tübingen school of sceptical scriptural studies, but also of numerous philosophers of religion deeply invested in the projects of modernity, I am privileged to participate in the creation of a department of Islamic Theology whose symbolic struggles may well illustrate, if not always illuminate, the insider/outsider binary whose real or imagined existence is the focus of our deliberations at this conference.

1 Islamic Theology at Tübingen, Germany

It was in 2011 that the University of Tübingen took the decision to establish a Center for Islamic Theology, a new academic unit dedicated to the study of Islam, intended to be equivalent to its two existing faculties of Protestant and Catholic Theology. This was based on the 2010 recommendation of the German Science and Humanities Council (Wissenschaftsrat),[3] followed by the federal government's approval.

On the basis of this initiative, departments or institutes of Islamic Theology were created not only in Tübingen, but in Osnabrück, Münster, Frankfurt am Main, Giessen, Erlangen, Paderborn and now the Humboldt University in Berlin. From the government and provincial perspective, the published intention was to ensure parity between the use of taxpayer's funds in support of training institutions for the country's major religions: the older Catholic and Protestant faculties reflecting Germany's historic religious experience, with the addition of Islamic theology; a response to the new demographic reality of a diversifying German society. From the point of view of Muslim communities, the new institutions have

3 "Recommendations on the Advancement of Theologies and Sciences concerned with Religions at German Universities, January 2010," Wissenschaftsrat, accessed October 28, 2023, https://www.wissenschaftsrat.de/download/archiv/9678-10_engl.html.

been welcomed not only as a symbol of acceptance, but also as an opportunity to intensify the quality and quantity of Muslim leadership in the German context.[4]

In the specific case of the Tübingen initiative, and to varying degrees in the case of the other institutions also, three guiding principles have defined this endeavour of rooting Islamic theology in German academe: (1) balance between theory and practice; (2) dialogue between traditional Islamic disciplines and social sciences as well as Oriental Studies; and (3) serious engagement with the interfaith context. Here I would like to briefly reflect on these three principles.

2 Balance between Theory and Practice

What is meant by a balance between theory and practice is that not only do we train theologians, but also teachers of Islam for German public schools as well as future staff for the spiritual care sector. Theology, of course, is that academic discipline which, while remaining alert to the larger intellectual trends of the contemporary academy, seeks to provide outcomes for the lived pastoral reality of faith communities, as well as developing philosophical tools to allow it to make sense of a rapidly changing world. German universities have maintained a historic tradition of embedding theology deeply within state universities, with a view to providing thinkers and also faith leaders who can practically impact their parish communities. This has roots deep in local history, in an often troubled past when relations between communities were strained and the need for direct and meaningful ethical guidance from church leaders was acute.

With a range of study programmes at both undergraduate (BA) and postgraduate (MA and PhD) level, our Center for Islamic Theology, while supporting around 200 students, and with specialists working in every important area of Islamic theology, including scripture, law, systematic theology, mysticism, and history, seeks to maintain this concern for public impact and utility.[5] Many of our graduates work in public sector roles, particularly in education and spiritual care, and are in a unique position to shape and guide younger members of Mus-

4 For a detailed account of the establishment of Islamic Theology as a new academic discipline at German Universities, see for instance, Bekim Agai and Armina Omerika, "Islamic Theological Studies in Germany: A Discipline in the Making", in *The Piety of Learning: Islamic Studies in Honor of Stefan Reichmuth*, ed. Michael Kemper and Ralf Elger (Leiden: Brill, 2017), 330–57.

5 For the current BA and MA study programmes offered at the Center for Islamic Theology, University of Tübingen, see "Study Programs," Center for Islamic Theology, Eberhard Karls Universität Tübingen, accessed October 28, 2023, https://uni-tuebingen.de/en/faculties/center-for-islamic-theology/study/study-programs/.

lim communities as they seek to define their relationship with wider German society. We are, in that sense, eminently and centrally pastoral.

Germany's growing Muslim population in many respects maintains a set of responses to modernity rooted in countries of origin. Hence in the case of Turkish communities, for instance, the variegated responses to Turkey's republican experiment, which provide religious markers for quite segregated populations, are largely present in the Federal Republic: hence there are German Diyanet representatives, Sufi orders, Süleymanci pietists, Gülenists, modernists, and Ottoman nostalgics, alongside other Muslim communities stemming from the Balkans, North Africa, and the Middle East. To this mix is added the complex set of demands and promises offered by membership of a German culture which is complexly Christian and secular. The theological enterprise to be pursued in the new academic hubs must, therefore, be open to exploring Islamic civilisation's strong but sometimes contested normative responses to the challenges of minority existence, to internal Muslim heterogeneity, and also to the myriad intellectual and moral challenges posed to Islamic truth claims by the modern project. The new centres thus provide scholarly and pedagogic spaces which transcend the parochial differentiations of Muslim communities. They further facilitate the construction of classically-resourced Islamic models of leadership, which allow these economically and politically disadvantaged communities to operate with a degree of unity, if not unanimity.

This challenge, which permits a degree of convergence between state and faithful agendas for a more unified Muslim representation and training, requires a strong presence of contextually-rooted theologies. Most German Muslims are heirs to the Maturidi theological legacy and the Hanafi legal-liturgical tradition, which Turkish republican – and also Bosnian – thought has often cited as the basis for the creation of a modern Islamic rationalism or empiricism, through an appropriation which is hoped to prove fruitful in dealing with Enlightenment rationalism and utilitarian and natural-law conceptions of moral life and the responsibility of individual citizens and religious corporate bodies. One could point to the pioneering nineteenth-century Maktab-i Nuwwab in Sarajevo (the Sharia School for Judges), or as the Austro-Hungarians called it, Scherijatische Richter Schule, as a prototype for resourcing Hanafi-Maturidi methods in response to the exigencies of Muslim life under European Christian rule.

This positioning of Maturidism as the optimal Muslim space for a dialogue with a modernity which is presumed to be rationalising and severed from textual revelation invites further research and philological processing of the enormous but still under-explored Maturidi literature. In Tübingen recently we published the first reader of *Maturidi Theology*, which presents Arabic texts with annotated

English translations to facilitate access to this tradition.[6] Other initiatives serving Maturidi thought are also planned. But this textual accessing is only a preliminary to the significant challenge of appropriating the heritage to serve as a conversation partner with Kantian and postmodern epistemologies and ethical deontology. The result might in some respects recall the twentieth-century neo-Thomist philosophies of Jacques Maritain (1882–1973), Frederick C. Copleston (1907–1994) and others who used the more philosophical dimensions of the writings of Aquinas as a basis for propounding a foundationalist system intelligible to the increasingly unyielding positivism of academic philosophy. As this ambitious project unfolds some are evincing the hope that many of the travails with modernity experienced in the mainstream Islamic world, where academic freedom is often seriously curtailed by regime policy, might be overcome. The German experiment would thus provide an institutional infrastructure allowing evolutions of a far more than simply German significance.

The purpose, however, cannot be merely abstract and metaphysical. Evidently morality, including any challenging ethic of encounter with the religious Other, must be grounded in sound theology if it is to be intellectually coherent and acceptable to base communities. The metaphysics must be generative of a practical theology. Islam is a religion of orthodoxies, broadly speaking, but also a religion of orthopraxies, with a rich panoply of ethico-legal life-patterns which shape the existence of believing men and women, taking them from self-orientation to an openness towards transcendence and virtue. Thus, for instance, in our department we were happy to co-organise an international interfaith conference on green theologies (Cambridge, 2019), in which leading Muslim and Christian theologians explored ways in which the re-sacralising of humanity's experience of the natural world might offer a strategy for coping with climate change. The proceedings in a sense showcase the modern Muslim capacity to engage thoughtfully with Christian and secular wisdom in the context of a shared contemporary crisis.[7]

Other such areas of collaboration and the creative exploration of difference could also be cited. The German situation of Islamic theology in institutional juxtaposition with other faculties of theology has allowed the transcendence of traditional Orientalist textual work, into a new space within the Western academy, in which Muslims are permitted to work academically within their own intellectual space, rather than submit in a sometimes notably colonial way to paradigms of external origin. This allows practical social impacts of a kind not historically

6 Lejla Demiri, Philip Dorroll and Dale J. Correa, eds., *Māturīdī Theology: A Bilingual Reader* (Tübingen: Mohr Siebeck, 2022).
7 Lejla Demiri, Mujadad Zaman and Tim Winter, eds., *Green Theology: Emerging 21st Century Muslim and Christian Discourses on Ecology* (Tübingen: Mohr Siebeck, 2024).

sought by Orientalism, whose historic mission to interpret and perhaps control Eastern cultures in an imperial age has shrivelled, and has not been saliently replaced by a discourse of Muslim identity constructed to facilitate the internal Muslim policy of European nation states.

3 Traditional Islamic Disciplines in Dialogue with Social Sciences and Oriental Studies

I have suggested that the toleration of a space for Muslim insider discourse, paralleling that historically allowed for Christian theology, represents a very significant expansion and diversification of the Humboldtian episteme. Needless to say, it has not gone unchallenged. However, the evident right of non-Christian communities to a habitus within the academy, given that since the Westphalian settlement the public funding of Protestant and Catholic theology has been part of the German constitutional landscape, raises important questions about the curriculum. Evidently Islamic theology in a modern university setting must adopt a hermeneutic of openness. Every question and perspective must be respectfully considered. A University department cannot be a seminary, presuming a certain credal compliance, even though accountability to faith communities must be ultimately secured through community participation in appointment processes.[8]

This openness is relatively easy to procure in an Islamic context. Maturidi texts, for instance, insist on the need for rational proof of God and His qualities, and this tradition of *kalam* philosophical theology grew from Islamic civilisation's capacity to accept the challenge of the Aristotelian-Platonic symphony which it inherited from its predecessors. As John Walbridge has shown in his book *The Caliphate of Reason*, Islamic thought is intensely hospitable to *ʿaql*, ratio; he sees this as one of the distinctive features of the classical madrasa tradition before modernity imposed either fundamentalist or simple pietistic priorities in many Muslim spaces.[9] There is a sense in which a re-engagement with logic, syllogism and challenges to religion's base assumptions is a re-activation of one of the most suc-

8 For the role and function of the Advisory Council (Beirat) of the Center for Islamic Theology at the University of Tübingen, see "Advisory Council," Center for Islamic Theology, Eberhard Karls Universität Tübingen, accessed November 22, 2023, https://uni-tuebingen.de/en/faculties/center-for-islamic-theology/center/advisory-council/.

9 John Walbridge, *God and Logic in Islam: The Caliphate of Reason* (Cambridge: Cambridge University Press, 2011).

cessfully formative processes and experiences which led to the medieval Muslim curriculum.

This complex return to *ratio* in nuanced conversation with revelation has proved fairly straightforward to champion in our new departments because they are independent. Whereas Catholic faculties, for instance, require licensing in various ways from Rome and the local episcopal hierarchy (many will recall the difficulties experienced by Hans Küng in Tübingen), Islam has no magisterium, but favours a radically de-centred model of religious authority. For some moderns this forms part of its ongoing appeal, and much Western Muslim theology makes full use of it: one could cite the Islamic theologies of Sherman Jackson, Ingrid Mattson, Tim Winter, and Charles Upton as influential examples.

Without sacraments there need be no priesthood, and therefore no structured authority, despite the quasi-ecclesiastical appearance of religious order in some modern Muslim nation-states. And this facilitates our task, insofar as an Islamic theological faculty in a modern European university is not dependent on licensing and inspection by a hierarchy claiming privileged access to the true interpretation of the deposit of faith and of the purport of scripture. The representative structures of Muslim communities in Europe are essentially political and social in their agendas and claim no right of doctrinal or jurisprudential oversight. The Muslim Council of Britain, for instance, seeks to shape a Muslim contribution to the public conversation, but claims no jurisdiction in internal religious discourses, still less to offer guidance on the proper symbiosis of secular and sacred knowledge. So here in the United Kingdom, for example, there are twenty-six Deobandi seminaries. In contrast with Anglican or Catholic equivalents, these are entirely self-regulating, determining their own curriculum and hermeneutic strategies, although they may operate within informal consensual partnerships, and exchange staff and insights on the application of classical curricula.[10]

In the German context, each of our institutes, while embedded in existing and sometimes quite anciently-established university ecosystems, similarly charts its own path through the jungle of contemporary social and philosophical questions. In this way German Islam can be claimed to echo Islam's recurrent historic patterns of the accommodation of diversity and the indulgence of minority or idiosyncratic views, a habit documented in Thomas Bauer's book *Die Kultur der Ambiguität*.[11] Muslims understand the inauguration of a theological world of difference and in-

---

10 For more on these seminaries, see for instance, Haroon Sidat, "Between Tradition and Transition: An Islamic Seminary, or *Dar al-Uloom* in Modern Britain", *Religions*, 9 (2018): 314, https://doi.org/10.3390/rel9100314.

11 Thomas Bauer, *Die Kultur der Ambiguität: Eine andere Geschichte des Islams* (Berlin: Verlag der Welt Religionen, 2011).

ternal conversations, unregulated by any magisterium stronger than a vaguely-articulated consensus, *ijmāʿ*, as one key contribution of Islam to monotheistic history. In some respects, it recalls certain forms of Judaism or the radical Protestantism of the kind which has flourished in Scotland: scripture alone is authoritative, and variant inspirations about its sense are, by and large, tolerated.

Nonetheless, no higher education institute can ignore the force of student interest. German Islam is on the whole attentive to tradition, and students in our institutions reflect this. They do not enrol in order to be trained in allegedly objective outsider perceptions. Indeed, recent cultural shifts often encourage students to prioritise insider narratives, as being possessed of greater intrinsic authenticity, distanced from the allegedly colonial subjection to a hegemonic Western episteme. But despite this student preference, the decision in the new German departments has been in favour of a range of creative and still experimental hybridisations with the regnant German *wissenschaftliche* paradigm, including the approaches of Religious Studies and Orientalism, which in many ways consider German universities as their place of birth. A hybrid approach is, moreover, inexorable, given that the wider universities impose appointment criteria which require that primary academic training lies within the Occidental paradigm. Where this is Orientalist – as it typically is, and if we are to believe Wael Hallaq the term is by no means a simply abusive one – then we are presented with an interesting laboratory experiment in which engaged Muslim academics who have deeply internalised objectivist and Orientalist approaches to texts and traditions interrogate those paradigms from within. The question then becomes: Are we Western academics exorcising the spirit of Kant and Humboldt in a return to a putative ancestral authenticity? Or are we still Orientals, eligible objects of the academy's gaze, using academic technologies to better proclaim God's glory? Of course, as we all breathe the air of deconstruction, such a simple binary cannot apply. Each academic and pedagogical decision is considered on the basis of the scholar's personal integration of self, context, knowledge and perception. There is no single resolution, only a kaleidoscope of applications of the individual self.

In practice, these academics, who are typically invited or expected to develop citizenship-friendly interpretations of the complex Muslim inheritance, often find that locating relevant and liberative dimensions *within* rather than *in conflict* with the inherited deposit of faith is startlingly easy. So, in our six different study programmes currently offered at Tübingen's Center for Islamic Theology, both at BA and MA levels, the courses range from classical Islamic disciplines such as Systematic Theology, Philosophy, Prophetic tradition, Scriptural Exegesis, Islamic law, Arabic language, Legal Theory and Ethics. Yet these cohabit with an equally strong Humanities focus including Intellectual and Social History, Islamic Art and

Aesthetics, Interfaith Studies, History of Education, and so forth. Finally, practical studies form part of the curriculum for those in the educational and chaplaincy degrees and include Pedagogy and Spiritual Care, and empirical research in religion and education.

To speak, in this effectively pastorally-directed pedagogical environment, of an Islamic theological commitment to equality and justice, however, is not to claim that every culture defines those concepts identically. By definition the modern Western elites define them in a manner which reflects a European heritage of the Enlightenment, shaped by Locke, Hayek, Popper, Rawls and others. Evidently Muslims working in this Western habitat must be entirely fluent in that language, and respect it for its achievements, particularly in securing the post-war European settlement, with its various human rights conventions. However, a contemporary alertness to the parochiality of the European, and the immanent risk of coloniality, must move Islamic theology beyond an easy subservience to these definitions of what constitutes a universal, towards a more up-to-date and non-Eurocentric acknowledgement of the right of different narratives to determine their own universals. The claim, made by some Muslims sceptical of the new departments of Islamic theology, that they exist simply to evolve discourses of assimilation and compliance, is best refuted by pointing to the new and inclusive culture of a multi-epistemic university, which regards the narrative of linear progress towards modern Western elite definitions of universality as colonial and demeaning.

To vindicate the authenticity of the new departments, it is important to point to the opportunities which now exist for the proposing of a non-subaltern discourse of cultural and religious difference. Medieval Europeans determined the value of a narrative in terms of its proximity to Christian orthodoxy. It is essential that modern Europeans do not evaluate scholarly discourse about culture and values on the basis of its compliance with the current value set of European and implicitly Eurocentric elites. In theological language, we point to the Qur'anic statement that 'We have appointed a law and a way for each people' (Qur'an 5:48), and to the principle that 'Every people has been sent a guide' (Qur'an 13:7). For Maturidism, and not just for Ash'arism, a theistic subjectivism undermines brave universals, insisting that while mind and conscience may recognise ethics, these only become binding in the presence of textual revelation. Theologians point to possible convergences between this theistic subjectivism and a contemporary Western relativising of values. And here we note that while many journalists and politicians regard the current normativities of Europe as rooted in reason, the major philosophical movements of late modernity have dismissed this entirely. Our values, for many of the most recent thinkers, are simply our values, useful for their familiarity and consensus value. But they are certainly not universals.

Here again we see how Islamic theology can benefit from a nuanced awareness of contemporary intellectual culture. The triumphalism of Victorian discourses of the 'West and the Rest' is now impossible. Hence the collapse of classical Orientalism, accelerated by Edward Said[12] and more recently by Wael Hallaq.[13] The purpose of Islamic Studies cannot be the mapping of an obsolete but often picturesque culture which was necessarily trumped via a Spencerian social evolutionary process by the superior adaptive capacity of Western humanity. Still less can scholars resource the scientific racism which defined Islam as 'semitic' for much of the 20th century. Instead, Orientalism has largely reconfigured itself as a more modest project detached from the older colonial mindset. Today many Islamic Studies specialists, whether Muslim or not, can be identified as advocates, campaigning for migration rights, and greater democratisation in the Middle East.

This eclipse of the old Orientalist insider/outsider episteme, coupled with a more humble self-understanding by a Western elite abashed by the threat of climate change and other existential threats, is another factor which enlarges the space for Islamic theology in the university. The culture has turned strongly against colonial and supremacist thinking. Hence the question for Muslim thinkers is not: how can Islam be justified to European elites on terms recognised by those elites, but rather: how can the diverse Islamic inheritance become the basis for a non-colonial Islamic Studies whose episteme and historico-cultural aspirations are grounded in a non-Western environment, and whose purpose must always be ethical and reparative?

Many Muslim scholars consider this to be possible but practically impossible: since academic research and pedagogy rooted in non-Western and thus non-Humboldtian habits of mind are unlikely to pass muster in the modern university world, in which preferment and peer-review mechanisms impose considerable uniformity. Appeals to universals which are not modernity's universals are likely to be penalised in practice, although theoretically acknowledged. For instance, within the project of the St Andrews Encyclopaedia of Theology, where I serve as a senior editor for the Islam section,[14] it is not uncommon to find some junior Muslim scholars hesitating to contribute to the project which is interested in reflecting insider perspectives. This inhibition is based on the concern that articulating an engaged Muslim take on a given topic may have unfavourable consequences for one's future career. So for the moment, scholars in the new institutions tend to operate conven-

12 Edward W. Said, *Orientalism* (New York, NY: Pantheon Books, 1978).

13 Wael B. Hallaq, *Restating Orientalism: A Critique of Modern Knowledge* (New York, NY: Columbia University Press, 2018).

14 "St Andrews Encyclopaedia of Theology," University of St Andrews, accessed June 10, 2024, https://www.saet.ac.uk.

tionally, publishing in mainstream journals, and attending mainstream conferences. But it is the experience of most that the disciplinary rigour expected in Orientalist work, particularly in the editing of manuscripts and the historical contextualising of Islamic beliefs, imposes high and beneficial standards. Many do not wish to switch epistemes, but find the best of Western styles of work to be very congenial.

4 Interfaith Context

Islamic theology in Europe possesses the advantage of a shared Middle Eastern origin with Christianity, a heritage historically interpreted through the categories of Aristotelian and Platonic thought. To this importantly-shared rooting must be added the centuries of substantive interactivity: Thomas Aquinas' indebtedness to Ibn Rushd (Averroes), for instance, or the early *kalam* resourcing of the Christian philosophy of John Philoponus. Orientalist historians have documented this interplay in detail. But it is for contemporary theologians, alert to the risks of dichotomising and othering, to find exemplary, though not binding, precedent in premodern Christian and Muslim interaction.

At Tübingen, our Center for Islamic Theology seriously engages with our context in Germany and in the wider European environment. It maintains close ties with the Faculties of Catholic and Protestant Theology. In particular I would like to mention the name of the Lutheran theologian Christoph Schwöbel (1955–2021) who even after his migration from Tübingen to St Andrews, consistently supported our fledgling institution, not only out of a sense of neighbourliness and collegiality, but from the conviction that the Abrahamic theologies, historically divided by difficult histories, must explore new strategies of mutual fecundation if they are to locate shared strategies of response to the growth of chauvinism in Europe. It is in this spirit that since the early days of Islamic theology we have been closely cooperating with the Catholic and Protestant Theology Faculties in both teaching and research. This enables a cross-fertilisation not only between our respective traditions of commentary on the diverse Abrahamic heritage, but also between our rather different trajectories and experiences of negotiating a settlement with modernity. In Germany that settlement appeared fairly early, in Kant's fierce opposition to any confessional project within universities, and the subsequent creation of theological faculties, as opposed to seminaries; the debate, which is even a constitutional one in the Federal Republic, is still far from settled, and is becoming a more contested space in an increasingly secular German environment. Engaging with the ways in which that intense local binary has been understood and resolved has been an important and enriching element as we seek to create an academically-responsible *Glaubenslehre* for Islam in the heart of its university system.

One of the early fruits of this interaction with the older theological faculties has been the recently established joint MA degree in Interfaith Studies, which also includes Jewish Studies.[15] Thus, our students are in a position to explore all three Abrahamic faith traditions within this unique programme. The trialogue is enhanced, but not inhibited or co-opted, by the real or imagined ground rules of secular religious studies. Here we join the mainstream national and Western debate about the viability of faith-hospitable spaces in the public square and in national institutions. There is certainly a specifically Islamic strand within that debate, but we see ourselves as an augmentation to the already complex range of settlements with the secular academy, a fluid and ongoing dialogue which, responsibly conducted, can only intensify the academic standards of both sides.

5 Scriptural Reasoning as a Case Study

What contemporary academic practices might prove congenial for this bridge-building, dialogical and socially-reparative style of theology which our faculties seem invited to promote? We have suggested that the older triumphalist narratives which place Europe at the summit of an evolutionary process are not generally regarded as defensible, and may be experienced as repugnantly colonial. Young people are unlikely to apply to institutions where they are told that their culture is inferior, and that salvation lies in converting to the social beliefs of dominant elites. But they need to be clear that they are not being offered a seminary or madrasa curriculum either, or anything like it. The agenda must therefore seek contemporary academic practices which do not disable Muslim faith commitments or social visions, but which nonetheless expect a high degree of attentiveness to difference.

One such method which we at Tübingen have found particularly helpful has been that of Scriptural Reasoning, familiarly abbreviated to SR. This is a strategy of re-reading scriptural foundational texts with an eye to detecting contemporary applications. But whereas modernist readings typically attempt to massage the texts to make them comply with current values, Scriptural Reasoning relativises and parochialises modernity, while accepting a kind of pragmatism in the selec-

15 See "Theologien interreligiös - Interfaith Studies - Master," Eberhard Karls Universität Tübingen, accessed November 22, 2023, https://uni-tuebingen.de/studium/studienangebot/verzeichnis-der-studiengaenge/detail/course/theologien-interreligioes-interfaith-studies-master/.

tion of preferred exegetic outcomes. The intellectual ancestry of this is American, through John Dewey and C. S. Peirce. But the use of a pragmatism in exegesis began in the early 1990s with the creation of the Society for Textual Reasoning, a university-based forum for scholars of Modern Jewish Philosophy and scholars of Rabbinic texts to meet and study together. Led by Peter Ochs, Steven Kepnes and others, this found in a reading which sought reparative outcomes a convergence with Talmudic styles of reading which refused decisiveness, but celebrated ambivalence and polyvalence. These hermeneuts were soon joined by Christian theologians, such as David Ford and Daniel Hardy, leading to the creation of the Society of Scriptural Reasoning. Finally, Muslim theologians joined, their research often being platformed in the movement's house journal, *The Journal of Scriptural Reasoning*, located at the University of Virginia.[16]

The appeal of this method is clear. For many of us in Islamic theology, it offers a refreshing potential to broaden the field, so often inhibited by its philological and historiographic templates, by the inclusion of a significant awareness of wider philosophical and cultural realities in the academy. Oriental Studies has, as its name perhaps implied, often formed a silo or backwater, whose unresponsiveness to new methods and philosophies has been deeply frustrating to many who seek to study Islam or other putatively 'Oriental' cultures with a fresh openness to the larger cultural and ideational shifts in the university. The field has often been criticised for its archaism and its lack of consciousness of more contemporary methods and outlooks. And Muslims in the field are often no less guilty of a kind of Victorianism in the way they understand and internalise the rules for progression in the guild. Some also feel the need for deference to the fixed opposition of many to what is seen as the intrusion of a normative religious commitment.

In contrast to this old-school Orientalist stasis, the expanding universe of Scriptural Reasoning allows scholars to apply contemporary and even postmodern approaches without being restricted by the need to cite contemporary authorities in any programmatic or compliance-signalling way. Participants bring to the table their own confessional libraries, which may entail philological, historico-critical, theological or other preoccupations. No determinate outcome is expected or even hoped for. In this sense Scriptural Reasoning is a postmodern exercise, and is thus very congenial to the dominant mode of philosophical work in the university. However – and for many Muslims this is the critical point – it is hospitable to foundationalist perspectives also, provided always that these do not impose themselves as the architects of a unique favoured reading. As with Jewish

16 "Current Issue," The Journal of Scriptural Reasoning, accessed June 10, 2024, https://jsr.shanti.virginia.edu.

hermeneutics, although perhaps to a lesser extent, Islamic styles of scriptural reading, unaccountable to a centralised institution, have historically been almost indefinitely diverse. The major premodern Qur'anic commentaries invariably cite a range of possible meanings of each verse; the author may indicate a preference, but this is seldom proposed as decisive.

My personal experience with Scriptural Reasoning goes back to 2004 when I began my postgraduate studies in Cambridge, as I was initiated into SR by an exceptional circle of Jewish, Christian and Muslim scholars, such as Peter Ochs, David Ford, and Tim Winter. In Tübingen, then, teamed up with my late colleague Christoph Schwöbel, I taught seven courses of Scriptural Reasoning seminars between 2015–2021, covering a range of topics, from 'Theological Anthropology' to 'Ecology', from 'Salvation' to 'Monotheism', from 'Time, God and Eternity' to 'Eschatology'. In 2022, our Scriptural Reasoning seminar, dedicated to the memory of Christoph, focused on the theme of 'Hope', this time co-taught by a number of distinguished Jewish, Christian and Muslim scholars. The same pattern was followed in 2023, hosting guest speakers among them Peter Ochs and David Ford, two founding fathers of SR.[17]

These seminars have been a fruitful platform for genuine religious and theological conversations for our students of Islamic and Christian theologies and beyond. To those schooled in the older rulebook of Islamic Studies this seems to introduce philosophical conventions and interests which violate the laws of the guild. To this the response of Muslim and other hermeneuts is the simple observation that classical Orientalism, with its canons of belonging and its stern procedures for what we might nowadays call the 'cancellation' of violators, seems less in tune with the mood of the modern academy than this modality of doing work with Muslim scriptures and texts. Readers of Scriptural Reasoning monographs and journals may even find themselves, as insider theologians, to be better placed near the heart of the university, than the classical Orientalists themselves. The turn to the subject, as many call it, upsets and destabilises traditional natural theologies, but no less thoroughly demolishes the Kantian reductionism which has maintained the firewall between religious studies and theology.

17 "Scriptural Reasoning 'Prophethood - Jewish, Christian and Muslim Perspectives'," Zentrum für Islamische Theologie (ZITh), Eberhard Karls Universität Tübingen, accessed November 21, 2023, https://uni-tuebingen.de/fakultaeten/zentrum-fuer-islamische-theologie/professuren/professur-fuer-islamische-glaubenslehre/news/#c1802740.

6 Conclusion

Here I have tried to summarise the first ten years of the infancy of Islamic theology in European academe with a special focus on the German University scene. For all the epistemological and institutional challenges, and sometimes one may even say prejudices, the foundations of this field have been established with the first fruits ripening, in both teaching and research, as testified by a growing number of popular study programmes, rigorous research projects and respectable publications. Following on these three foundational principles, namely a healthy balance between theory and practice; a dialogue between traditional Islamic disciplines and social sciences as well as Oriental Studies; and a genuine engagement with an interfaith context often sidelined by academic convention, one may regard the future of Islamic theology in Germany with a certain optimism.

Of Scriptural Reasoning in its trialogic modality, shaped by a further dialogue with secular modernity, David Ford speaks of

> the double, simultaneous intensity of both reasoning around scriptures and reasoning across the scriptural-secular boundary. To do one without the other limits the resources of possible wisdom. To do both together in mutual enhancement and critique could well shape vital contributions to the Islam-West encounter.[18]

It is this double, simultaneous intensity which should guide our work. Older traditions of editing and translating, and of historical analysis, even reduction, are not threatened by this new space of what Ford calls 'interactive particularity', which fully encounters modern secular wisdom. Instead, they are complemented and even affirmed. Here Orientalism finds its contemporary vocation and resignification: the supply of the edited and comprehended discursive tradition of Islam, which more contemporary methods then engage, not to close, but to open up the episteme.

The Qur'an insists that 'the differences of your languages and colours' are a blessed Divine indicant (Qur'an 30:22); and the growing Muslim demographies of Europe, heirs to lands and traditions of immense diversity, seem well-placed, when well-led, to assist Europe in its present historic transformation into a multiethnic and multi-confessional continent. Whatever future evolutions we may expect, European Islamic theology thus becomes a discipline of far more than purely academic significance.

---

18 David F. Ford, "Developing Scriptural Reasoning Further," in *Scripture, Reason, and the Contemporary Islam-West Encounter: Studying the "Other," Understanding the "Self"*, ed. Basit Bilal Koshul and Steven Kepnes (New York, NY: Palgrave Macmillan, 2007), 201–19, 215.

Lejla Demiri is Professor of Islamic Doctrine at the Center for Islamic Theology, University of Tübingen. She received her PhD from the University of Cambridge (2008), and held post-doctoral fellowships at Trinity Hall, Cambridge (2007–10) and the Free University of Berlin (2010–2). Her research explores systematic theology, intellectual history of Islam and Muslim-Christian theological encounters. She is the author of *Muslim Exegesis of the Bible in Medieval Cairo* (Brill, 2013), and co-editor of *The Future of Interfaith Dialogue* (with Y. Said; CUP, 2018), *Early Modern Trends in Islamic Theology* (with S. Pagani; Mohr Siebeck, 2019) and *Theological Anthropology in Interreligious Perspective* (with M. Zaman, et al.; Mohr Siebeck, 2022). She served as Section Editor for *Christian-Muslim Relations. A Bibliographical History (1500– 1900)* (Brill, 2012–2024), and is currently Senior Editor (Islam) of *St Andrews Encyclopaedia of Theology* (2019–present).

Bibliography

Agai, Bekim, and Armina Omerika. "Islamic Theological Studies in Germany: A Discipline in the Making." In *The Piety of Learning: Islamic Studies in Honor of Stefan Reichmuth*, edited by Michael Kemper and Ralf Elger, 330–57. Leiden: Brill, 2017.

Bauer, Thomas. *Die Kultur der Ambiguität: Eine andere Geschichte des Islams*. Berlin: Verlag der Welt Religionen, 2011.

Eberhard Karls Universität Tübingen. "Advisory Council." Center for Islamic Theology. Accessed November 22, 2023. https://uni-tuebingen.de/en/faculties/center-for-islamic-theology/center/advisory-council/.

Eberhard Karls Universität Tübingen. "Scriptural Reasoning 'Prophethood – Jewish, Christian and Muslim Perspectives'." Zentrum für Islamische Theologie (ZITh). Accessed November 21, 2023. https://uni-tuebingen.de/fakultaeten/zentrum-fuer-islamische-theologie/professuren/professur-fuer-islamische-glaubenslehre/news/#c1802740.

Eberhard Karls Universität Tübingen. "Study Programs." Center for Islamic Theology. Accessed October 28, 2023. https://uni-tuebingen.de/en/faculties/center-for-islamic-theology/study/study-programs/.

Eberhard Karls Universität Tübingen. "Theologien interreligiös – Interfaith Studies – Master." Accessed November 22, 2023. https://uni-tuebingen.de/studium/studienangebot/verzeichnis-der-studiengaenge/detail/course/theologien-interreligioes-interfaith-studies-master/.

Demiri, Lejla, Philip Dorroll and Dale J. Correa, eds. *Māturīdī Theology: A Bilingual Reader*, Tübingen: Mohr Siebeck, 2022.

Demiri, Lejla, Mujadad Zaman and Tim Winter, eds. *Green Theology: Emerging 21st Century Muslim and Christian Discourses on Ecology*. Tübingen: Mohr Siebeck, 2024.

Ford, David F. "Developing Scriptural Reasoning Further." In *Scripture, Reason, and the Contemporary Islam-West Encounter: Studying the "Other," Understanding the "Self"*, edited by Basit Bilal Koshul and Steven Kepnes, 201–19. New York, NY: Palgrave Macmillan, 2007.

Ghazālī, Al-. *The Ninety-Nine Beautiful Names of God*. Translated by David B. Burrell and Nazih Daher. Cambridge: The Islamic Texts Society, 2004.

Hallaq, Wael B. *Restating Orientalism: A Critique of Modern Knowledge*. New York, NY: Columbia University Press, 2018.

Said, Edward W. *Orientalism*. New York, NY: Pantheon Books, 1978.

Sidat, Haroon. “Between Tradition and Transition: An Islamic Seminary, or *Dar al-Uloom* in Modern Britain.” *Religions* 9 (2018), 314. https://doi.org/10.3390/rel9100314.

The Journal of Scriptural Reasoning. “Current Issue.” Accessed June 10, 2024. https://jsr.shanti.virginia.edu.

University of St Andrews. “St Andrews Encyclopaedia of Theology.” Accessed June 10, 2024. https://www.saet.ac.uk.

Walbridge, John. *God and Logic in Islam: The Caliphate of Reason*. Cambridge: Cambridge University Press, 2011.

Wissenschaftsrat. “Recommendations on the Advancement of Theologies and Sciences concerned with Religions at German Universities, January 2010.” Accessed October 28, 2023. https://www.wissenschaftsrat.de/download/archiv/9678-10_engl.html.

Diwakar Acharya

Knowing and Thinking about the Ultimate in Hindu Theology: The Issues of Transcendence and Immanence

1 Introduction: The God of Gods

Success in this world and attainment of heaven in the other are for many people the goals of human life but classical Indian religious traditions, not only Hindu[1] but also Buddhist and Jain, see freedom from the transmigratory existence, from the cycle of death and rebirth, as the ultimate wellbeing, and define it as the ultimate goal of human existence. None of these aims is attainable, from theological and normative perspective, without knowing the ultimate truth, its nature, and our relationship with it. Therefore, ancient Indian thinkers have thought and taught about the ultimate in various theological, metaphysical, and philosophical contexts, looking at it from different perspectives.

The ultimate can be conceptualised as something foundational, fundamental, and irreducibly real, for example, the four or five elements, or atoms. It can be that which transcends all in existence, phenomenal or noumenal. It can be a transformative truth or perspective that is normatively or soteriologically most important such as the truth of dependent origination or emptiness in Buddhism. It can also be the One that controls and runs the world such as the God; the Time according to some; the destiny, or the eternal Ritual, or Karma according to others. We encounter all these in Indian traditions, but as it would not be possible to cover all of these here, I will focus in this paper on the theological and philosophical notions of Brahman, Puruṣa and Ātman as the Ultimate cosmic principle and the essence of every sentient being.

Ancient Indians are well known for plurality and diversity of their gods, worldviews, rituals, beliefs, and customs, elaborated in their equally diverse scriptures and discourses found in them. It is not surprising that people in such polytheistic environment make a hierarchy of gods they worship, and identify

1 The term Hindu as a reference to all classical Indian religious traditions except Buddhism and Jainism is a convenient neologism, but it has a longer history as an adjective qualifying people and things to the other side of the Indus River as see from the side of Iran. See, e.g., Bihani Sarkar, "Where Ants Dig up Gold: 'India', Selfhood and the Myths Manufacturing a Nation," in *British Academy Review* 30, (Summer 2017): 46–7.

https://doi.org/10.1515/9783111454658-004

one among many Gods as the highest or the most powerful that supports and governs the world of sentient and insentient beings.

If we enter the early Vedic world of the *Ṛgveda* (RV hereafter),[2] we find inspired Vedic poets praising one or the other god as the most important one in terms of ritual and cosmic or any other power—as the strongest, mightiest, dearest god, or the most invited god, and also as the God over gods (*deveṣv adhidevaḥ*[3]), the God among gods (*devatrā devaḥ*[4]), the one God alone (*deva ekaḥ*[5]), and so on. At all times the masses in the Indic world subscribe to this approach, and name one or the other god as the Ultimate according to their choice, inclination or devotion, placing other gods lower in hierarchy; they worship many gods but identify one as the all-powerful.

Initially, as it appears, they had not coined a fixed name to refer to the Ultimate God. In the hymn of Golden Embryo[6] (RV X.121), they resort to a rhetoric of lamentation as they are unable to give him a name. They do describe his functions or actions, and in a refrain repeatedly ask who is the God functioning this way to whom they should pay homage with their oblation. The hymn says, the Golden Embryo evolved in the beginning, and born the lord of what came to be, he alone then existed. By his greatness, he alone became the king of the breathing, blinking, moving world of bipeds and quadrupeds. The Himalayas in their greatness and the sea together with the rivers belong to him. His are all directions, zenith and nadir are his arms. He is the progenitor of earth, the firm foundations. He is the god over gods, the life of the gods (*devānāṃ asuḥ*). He engendered heaven, he engendered the gleaming, lofty waters, and oversaw cosmic waters giving birth to the ritual. He made the mighty heaven and earth firm, steadied the sun, the firmament, and measured out the airy realm in the intermediate space. He supports the earth and the heavens, and all including the gods honour his command. He is the giver of breath, and strength also. Immortality is his shadow, death as well.[7]

In the middle of these descriptions, nine out of ten stanzas of this hymn repeat: "who is the god to whom we should do homage with our oblation?" The trouble faced by the poet of this hymn is that the God he has visualised is so great

2 RV = Ṛgveda. *Die Hymnen des Ṛigveda*, ed. Th. Aufrecht. 2 vols., Indische Studien 6–7 (Berlin: Ferd. Dümmler's Verlagsbuchhandlung, 1861–3).

3 Cf., e.g., RV X.121.8.

4 Cf., e.g., RV I.50.10.

5 Cf., e.g., RV X.51.1.

6 Apparently, it is a description of the Sun at the centre of the cosmos as the ultimate cause of the cosmos.

7 Cf., *The Rigveda: The Earliest Religious Poetry of India*, trans. Stephanie W. Jamison and Joel P. Brereton, 3 vols. (Oxford: Oxford University Press, 2014), 1593–4.

that he cannot be contained in one name. In the RV, as Jamison & Brereton remark,

> By invoking, varying, and meaningfully placing gods' names in their verses and by echoing the sounds of those names, the poets bring about the presence of the gods, their epiphany. More than in any other single feature, the essential nature of a deity is expressed in the god's name. The god is who the god is because the god obeys the truth embedded in that name.[8]

Thus, inability to contain the Ultimate in a name was the problem of the poets who envisioned it. For some time, they continued asking rhetorical questions, using a descriptive term, or presenting enigmatic riddles, but it seems, they were having in mind at times the Sun god with different functions, or the Sacred fire, Varuṇa, or Indra at others.

However, soon towards the end of the Early Vedic period, as evidenced in the first and last book of the RV itself and in other Vedic Saṃhitās, Vedic seers made a leap and started to see 'the One' not among many gods but behind all gods, one and the same, and all others as different manifestations of that one.

Poet Medhya Kāṇva, the seer of RV VII.58.2, sees the One as if it is a metaphysical principle as he describes Him deploying powerful similes: "Just one fire is kindled in many forms; just one sun has projected through all. Just one dawn radiates over this whole (world). In truth just One has developed into this whole (world)."[9]

2 The Maker of Everything

The seer of RV I.164.46 reports: they call him Indra, Mitra, Varuṇa, Agni, then also that, he is the divine well-feathered bird. He is one but the wise people with poetic vibrancy call him in many ways; they call him Agni, Yama, and Mātariśvan. This implies that any god named in one or the other way, uttering a designation or an epithet, is simply a representation of one aspect of the Only God. A name is simply a verbal handle (cf. ChU VI.4.1)[10] to get a handle on a specific manifesta-

---

8 *Rigveda*, 35.
9 *Rigveda*, 1141.
10 ChU = *Chāndogya Upaniṣad*. See V. P. Limaye and R. D. Vadekar, *Eighteen Principal Upaniṣads* (Poona: Vaidika Saṃśodhana Maṇḍala, 1958), 68–173; For a translation, see Patrick Olivelle, *The Early Upaniṣads. Annotated Text and Translation* (Oxford: Oxford University Press, 1998).

tion of the One Ultimate behind, the sole cause and source of diversity of the divine as well as the mortal world. As RV X.81–82 describe,[11] he is the Maker of Everything (Viśvakarman); the carpenter and smith of creation who fashioned the world. He creates all and everything in this and all possible worlds. He is the priest engaged in the cosmic sacrifice pouring out all living beings. He is the cosmic sacrifice: simultaneously the agent, object, and process of it, and sacrifices himself to perpetually create and recreate the world. He has his eye on everything. He alone produces heaven and earth, he forges them together with his arms, he has eyes and face turned in every direction, his arms and feet moving in every direction (cf. RV X.81.2–3). He conceals those of the past as he enters the later generations (cf. RV X.81.1). He is vast in mind and power; he is the just and vast distributor of the rewards of our deeds. He manifests to the highest, greatest, subtlest, and fullest. He is the father and progenitor of all, he knows all the domains and all living beings, he is the one alone who gives names to the gods (RV X.82.2); and by implication, to all those he has casted in the manifest phenomenal existence. He is the Lord of Speech (Vācaspati), specifically the lord of Truthful Speech (Brahmaṇaspati), thus he is the omniscient thinker and the omnipotent actor.

3 The Lord of Creatures

In the Middle Vedic Brāhmaṇa texts, we can observe that alongside various rituals the conception of the Ultimate develops further, and as it becomes now difficult to see the Sun god or any other exalted divinity as the Ultimate, the seers name the Maker of Everything, the newly understood Ultimate, as Prajāpati, "the Lord of Creatures." He has macrocosmic and microcosmic bodies, and thus he is greater than the greatest and subtler than the subtlest. As the Vedic ritualists of the Brāhmaṇas (the Vedic exegetical texts) narrate, Prajāpati was alone in the beginning and had independent will. He desired to be embodied, to have the world with sentient and insentient beings for his body, and thus, diversified himself into the world. He does it eternally and makes everything, transmuting himself into various beings in different levels, enters them as their inner essence, soul or self, introduces order and rules for them, and remains at the top of everything as the just supervisor, witnessing operations of all rules and laws including the law of karmic fruition and the autonomous system of ritual. He sets everything in motion or station.

11 For a full translation of these hymns, see *Rigveda*, 1513–7.

As Keith describes,

> he is constantly the creator, the ruler, and the preserver of the world and is accepted by every Brāhmaṇa of the period as being the lord of the world: he is, it may be added, without any ethical importance: the conception of him is purely intellectual, that of the unity of the universe, [. . .]. Of Prajapati's activities the most interesting are his relation as creator to the gods, to the Asuras, whose connexion is with the darkness and cunning, and to men. He is, however, much more than the mere universe: he is the unmeasured, the unexpressed, as opposed to the measured and the expressed in nature: he is the seventeenth beside the sixteen elements of the psychic organs: the thirty-fourth above the thirty-three gods. He is universal peace, the decider of disputes among the gods; he gives Indra his victorious prowess and his crown of victory.[12]

He is also equated with the altar, the body of the ritual (*yajña*) and its supermundane representation in various levels, with time (*kāla*) as the Year (*saṃvatsara*), also with the sacred truthful speech (*brahman*), and actually with many other entities of mythical, ritual, or metaphysic value.[13]

4 The Non-Existent, the Existent, and Beyond

In fact, no name including the Lord of Creatures can carry the weight of the Ultimate. Vedic poets, mystics, and exegetes, at least some of them, realised it as they became more contemplative. Thus, we find them replacing the Lord of Creatures (Prajāpati) with metaphysical principles such as the nameless and formless Non-Existent, or the primordial Existent, even before we enter the early Upaniṣadic works of the later Vedic periods. This metaphysical principle has multidimensional transmutations, for example, in its fervour of creation, it evolves into heat, water, and earth in the ontic sphere; into the cosmic order, truth, and ascetic power in the ethical sphere; and into speech, vital functions, and mind, and so on in the bodily sphere.[14]

---

12 Arthur Berriedale Keith, *The Religion and Philosophy of the Veda and Upanishads*, vol. 2, Harvard Oriental Series 32 (Cambridge, MA: Harvard University Press, 1925), 442–3. Reprint, Delhi: Motilal Banarsidass, 1970.

13 For these and other wide-ranging equations of the Lord of Creatures with cosmic, microcosmic, and ritualistic meso-cosmic realities in the Atharvaveda and Brāhmaṇa texts, see Keith, *Religion and Philosophy*, 444–5.

14 For an account of such transmutations of the Ultimate into metaphysical realities as found mainly in the *Jaiminīya Brāhmaṇa*, see Diwakar Acharya, "This World, in the Beginning, was Phenomenally Non-Existent: Āruṇi's Discourse on Cosmogony in the *Chāndogya Upaniṣad*." *Journal of Indian Philosophy* 44, no. 5 (November 2016): 848–52.

Even in the RV itself, the *Nāsadīyasūkta* (RV X.129) tries to go beyond metaphysical dichotomies and says, neither the non-existent, nor the existent existed at the primordial dawn; neither death nor deathlessness, nor time, nothing else beyond that was there. There then was the darkness of unknowability hidden by darkness. All this we call the cosmos was then a signless ocean, concealed by emptiness. There 'that One' breathed without wind by its independent will, born by the power of its own energy.

5 The Ultimate Brahman: Transcendence and Immanence

The Ultimate thus is the sole source of all diverse forms from where every entity springs forth and it is the repository where all including individual living beings go back. It is the basis that provides space and occasion for all to come into being but evades description. We may say, it is the 'it' that is encountered even before we predicate a thing and say 'it exists.' Every predication, designation, description, as a verbal handle can capture only one aspect of it. However, these too much depersonalized principles, though desire and resolve were still assigned to them, could not obviously whet everybody's palate and so were abandoned subsequently in the favour of the neuter term *brahman* which originally meant truthful speech, and covered a range of connotations such as prayer, Vedic sacred learning, and by extension the Holy Word, and the sacred in general. Because of epiphanic capabilities of the prayer, and also because of its earlier equation with Prajāpati, we can assume, it also implied to the One behind all gods.

On the other hand, as it appears, there were some other people with strong devotional feelings who could not think of depersonalizing the Ultimate at all, even at the transcendental level. They simplified the notion of 'the lord of creatures' simply in the notion of 'the man,' the primordial man (Puruṣa). As they saw Him (RV X.90), the primordial man covered the earth on all sides and then extended beyond. He alone is this entire world: he is what has come into being and also what is yet to come into being. He is the master of immortality when he climbs beyond this world. The world is his vastness/greatness, but he is more than that: a quarter of him makes all living beings, and three quarters of him has risen up beyond the world as the immortal. They continued parallelly adopting sophistications of new ways of thinking as much as possible, for example, Vedic gods Rudra and Viṣṇu found new interpretations and adherences, and got identified as the Ultimate Puruṣa, and in turn, Puruṣa is seen as having higher and lower natures, instead of forms, identified as the self-luminous cognising principle and the world of the dynamic materiality.

In the view of the early Upaniṣadic thinkers (cf. BĀU II.3),[15] Brahman the Ultimate has two forms: immortal and mortal, which can be as non-embodied and embodied, dynamic and static, and two halves of the truth. As they perceive, the essential core of the immortal is Puruṣa, the person, the principle that knows, thinks, cognises, perceives.[16]

Here we can observe that the Vedic seers are now thinking about the Ultimate in more complex ways in terms of metaphysics, and have realised that the Ultimate is not only immanent but also transcendent. Actually, in Brahman, they have found a theory of everything, it is the origin of everything. For example, in the social sphere of gods and humans, initially Brahman is alone as the priestly, the sacred. Feeling incomplete, in the fervour of diversification, it transmutes first as the mighty, the royal, then as the skilful, the class of common people, then as the serving class. But still it feels incomplete and transmutes again as Dharma, the social Law claimed to be constant, and he becomes complete and satisfied. There is a similar story concerning gender distinction and reproduction. Thus, Brahman is the being of beings, soul of souls, life of life, present in all as the substratum of existence/being.

Thus, by the time of the earliest Upaniṣads, we have six different concepts or models for reflection on the Ultimate: 1) as the God among gods, or the lord of gods, 2) as the God behind all gods, 3) as the creator and ruler of everything, 4) as the first being that becomes the world through self-sacrifice and transcends, that means, the immanent-cum-transcendent God, 5) as the metaphysical principle with dual nature, explained from cosmogonic point of view accepting the world as real, and 6) the same metaphysical principle explained from the cognitive-contemplative point of view, with strong apophatic denial of the world with focus on the transcendental.

These six concepts of the Ultimate based on the changing notions of Brahman and Puruṣa and Ātman, independently or in combination, inspired theological and philosophical developments in all traditions of Hinduism in various stages in the late Vedic age, in the age of the development of philosophical systems, and in the age of philosophical and theological exegesis. For example, we have some evi-

15 BĀU = *Bṛhad Āraṇyaka Upaniṣad*. See Limaye, *Eighteen Principal Upaniṣads*, 174–282; For a translation, see Olivelle, *The Early Upaniṣads*, 1998.

16 Cf., Diwakar Acharya, "*Néti néti*. Meaning and Function of an Enigmatic Phrase in the Gārgya-Ajātaśatru dialogue of *Bṛhad Āraṇyaka Upaniṣad* II.1 and II.3," *Indo-Iranian Journal* 56, no. 1 (January 2013): 18–20, especially footnote 27.

dence that the original theistic Śāṃkhya tradition[17] was rooted in Vedic theology and believed in the sentient and the insentient as the dual nature of the Ultimate Being. According to it, these two natures of Puruṣa evolve together combined, into everything in the world, creating a hierarchy down to the level of diverse individual beings in the coexistence of the embodied Puruṣa and his body. Thus, all and everything, all persons, according to this view, are like sparks or minion clones of that cosmic embodied person, retaining the dual nature of the embodied and his body. In the process of evolution, the body changes, but the purity of the sentient does not change in substance, even though its function and appearance changes. For them, the ultimate as the cosmic self is present as one but many as worldly beings.

We can reflect here on the propositions of various exegetical schools of Vedānta and also other philosophical systems. Śaṅkara (8th century CE) sees the God as an appearance of the Ultimate, perhaps the best or highest of all appearances but not the Ultimate as it is, the universally present fundamental metaphysical essence present in everything. For Śaṅkara, Brahman as the Ultimate transcends the world, but the world cannot independently exist, it appears/occurs in Brahman, therefore it is neither real nor unreal. The ultimate reality of Brahman is independent, it is like the water of ocean different from its whirlpools, aquatic animals and so on. As he thinks, the Ultimate truth cannot be experienced through our devotional relationship with God, though he acknowledges the value of such relationship in purification of one's mind-and-heart, but believes that such relationship can be blocking the all-encompassing, direct and non-dual experience of the ultimate. As he proposes, one can gain non-dual holistic awareness of the ultimate, after seeing the limits of human intellect and critically negating everything in the world, one by one, and seeing the ultimate as transcending all of them. This method of critical negation according to Śaṅkara will allow them at the end, sooner or later, to experience the transcendental as the foundation of everything, remaining unnegated in every negation, lying beyond name, form, and function or process which mask the reality by highlighting only one aspect and masking the rest. The moment man is awakened to this reality, he starts seeing the transcendent and the immanent as one and the same in two forms, infinite and finite, and becomes liberated in this life. This very much commits to the non-dualistic proposition of Yājñavalkya of the early Upaniṣadic ages.

17 This idea can be found reflected at places in the *Mahābhārata*, for example, in I.1.27–36 where the text describes that the Unmanifest Ultimate evolves in two ways into metaphysical realities and as divinities governing them. This can be found even in the *Bhagavad Gītā* (7.4–5).

On the other hand, Rāmānuja (11th century CE) argues, citing older exegetical works, that the word 'Brahman' denotes the superior-most Person, the Ultimate being, who is by nature free from all defilements and possesses a host of innumerable auspicious qualities of boundless excellence. According to him, the word Brahman is used everywhere in the scriptures in connection with the quality of greatness and exaltation, and greatness lies there where lies the boundless excellence of intrinsic self-nature and also the qualities; this is the primary meaning of the term. And, such a being is no one else but the Supreme Lord, therefore the word Brahman is primarily used in that very sense. When used in connection with anyone else other than him, the usage is metaphorical thanks to the connection of that being with a trifle of those qualities, because it is not appropriate to postulate many referents of a word. For example, the term Bhagavant primarily refers to the Supreme Lord and metaphorically to any individual being having defined divine qualities. Therefore, Rāmānuja says, precisely the Supreme Lord is Brahman, the object of everyone's spiritual quest, and all those who are sick of the threefold affliction should precisely seek to know him for the sake of immortality. (cf. *Śrībhāṣya* I.1.1).[18]

In his view, the Ultimate Brahman is different from non-sentient matter known through ordinary means of knowledge, perception and others, and also from the sentient souls, whether connected with or separated from matter. The Ultimate is free from even a shadow of imperfection of any kind. Thus, God, infinite sentient beings, and insentient primal matter are three independent irreducible realities, but these three are inseparable and God in the form of Lord Viṣṇu rules over the other two as he presides over the world, because he is an ocean of auspicious qualities. He is the sole cause of the entire universe that is his body, and constitutes the inner Self of all things (*Śrībhāṣya* II.1.1). Thus, the ruling lord is the soul of souls: the soul of the entire world comprised of sentient and insentient beings. As the Ultimate, he is the pure being, omnipotent and omniscient, and his purpose is always realised (cf. *Vedārthasaṃgraha*, prologue). He is the abode of Śrī, excellence personified, and sports with cosmic tasks like creation, maintenance, and absorption of all worlds. He has vowed to exclusively protect all classes of beings devoted to him (cf. *Śrībhāṣya*, the opening verse of benediction). As Rāmānuja explains, ocean is water as well as everything there: waves, foam, whirlpools, animals, plants, and so on which are different but inseparable from the ocean. Likewise, souls are modes or bodies of the supreme, so are the

18 Śrībhāṣya = Brahmasūtra-Śrībhāṣya of Sri Bhagavad Rāmānuja with the Śrutaprakāśikā of Śrī Sudarśanasūri, 2. vols. Chennai: Visishtadvaita Pracharini Sabha, 1989.

objects in the world. The same proposition of three irreducible reals in inseparable relation can be found in many Śaiva and Vaiṣṇava traditions, with the same believe that Śiva or Viṣṇu or Krishna is independent and reigns supreme presiding over everything and every process. Let me add here that we can easily relate the core of these propositions with the pre-Yājñavalka proposition of Brahman with two forms and Puruṣa with two natures, sentient and non-sentient, and inseparability of Brahman and its forms can be seen implied.[19]

Some other Śaiva and Vaiṣṇava traditions believe that God is the Ultimate, and the same irreducible three reals are there, but add that all sentient beings should serve him, because the Lord is capable of eternal damnation or elevation of them. He can free them, grant companionship, or keep them in bondage. This position can find support from the earliest notions of the Ultimate as the almighty ruler of the world. and the realist system of Nyāya-Vaiśeṣika can be aligned here which believes that there are atoms of different kinds serving as the building blocks of the world. Atoms, time, space, mind, individual sentient beings and God, they enumerate all as real, but assign special significance to the Supreme Self, the great God, who plays a crucial role in creation by connecting atoms and making composite things which are tangible, visible, and nameable; moving and functioning. Furthermore, the Supreme Self here supervises distribution of the rewards of the deeds of infinite sentient beings justly. However, they in principle believe that the Ultimate, the supreme Lord, is capable of doing things, not doing things, and doing things otherwise beyond normal rules (*kartuṃ akartum anyathākartum samarthaḥ*), nevertheless he abides by the rules he sets. He is the creator of all, the governor of all.[20]

6 Human Engagement with the Ultimate

As soon as we enter the Upaniṣadic world of abstraction and meditative cultivation, we are exposed to difficult questions which are beyond cosmogony but closer to human heart: If Brahman is the cosmic principle transmuted into every-

---

19 For a discussion of the Vedantic understanding of the relationship between the Ultimate Brahman and the creator God (*Īśvara*) in different schools, see Gérard Colas, "Evolution of Deism and Theism up to the 12th Century: Some Considerations," in *Viṣṇu-Nārāyaṇa: Changing Forms and the Becoming of a Deity in Indian Religious Traditions*, ed. Marcus Schmücker (Vienna: Austrian Academy of Sciences, 2023), 296–9.

20 For the Nyāya understanding of God and theistic argument, see, e.g. N. Guha, M. Dasti and S. Phillips. *God and the World's Arrangement: Readings from Vedanta and Nyaya Philosophy of Religion* (Indianapolis/Cambridge: Hackett Publishing Company, 2021), 41–62.

thing, what are we as a self-aware, knowing, thinking individual being? Or, how can we understand our core, if we are individual representations or reflections of the Ultimate; and our mind, speech, and vital functions are his expressions? How much we are different and how much not different from the Ultimate? What is the meaning of the spiritual quest if we are already the Ultimate? How can we relate ourself with the Ultimate, unite with him, or experience him? and so on.

The first solution to this we find in the form of a meditation on Brahman the Ultimate as Reality, that means, the Immanent. As Śāṇḍilya of Kuru-Pāñcāla, a forerunner of Yājñavalkya of Kosala-Videha teaches, one should meditate in one's lifetime that he is the subtler than the subtlest Puruṣa as if 'a grain of rice, or a grain of barley, or a grain of millet, or the smallest granule of millet' inside the [universal] body that is all-present and greater than the greatest. This ancient teaching distinguishes Puruṣa as the cosmic core represented or reflected in every being from *ātman* as the enduring body, and understands that Puruṣa as the sentient dwells inside *ātman*, the body of vitality. To be released from the individual's particular inner enduring body and be in the cosmic universal body, one should meditate in one's lifetime, or at least in the last moments, on the cosmic body (*ātman*) which is made of mind *(manomaya)*, has vital functions for its body-structure (*prāṇaśarīra*), light for its visual appearance (*bhārūpa*), *and* space for its body-expansion (*ākāśātman*); a body capable of changing its shape freely, has swiftness of mind (*manojavasa*), true imagination *(satyasaṃkalpa)* and true resolution (*satyadhṛti*); a body that partakes of all smells and all tastes, that holds sway over all the quarters and pervades all in the world; which is speechless *(avākka)* and intentless (*anādara*). 'That is my body, I shall obtain that after departing from here,' whoever has a determination in this way, no uncertainty is there for him. For, the individual person in this world is endowed with the volitional power (*kratu*), and with as much of this power one departs from this world, so much power (*kratu*) he comes to possess after entering the other world.[21]

Perhaps after a couple of centuries or less, Yājñavalkya has a slightly different idea of Ātman according to which Ātman is omnipresent like the space and is without any attribute in itself, but as things occur in omnipresent Ātman, its conditional attributes appear, and the best and most fundamental of such attributes are pure-being, pure-awareness, and pure-bliss. When things come together and a body is formed, Ātman serves as the core of that body, so Yājñavalkya believes. We see in this doctrine Puruṣa and Ātman merge into one: vitality is not different

---

21 Cf., ŚB X.6.3.1-2; ŚB = Śatapatha-Brāhmaṇa. The Çatapatha-Brâhmaṇa in the Mâdhyandina-Çâkhâ with Extracts from the Commentaries of Sâyaṇa, Harisvâmin, and Dvivedagaṅga. ed. Albrecht Weber (Leipzig: Otto Harrassowitz, 1924).

from self-luminosity; vital functions come out of the core when conditions are met. Yājñavalkya asked to experience this fundamental principle of Ātman in its purity, first through cataphatic but ultimately through apophatic awareness of one's own Self, once thus purified by way of dropping all attributes one after the other, one's self is no other than the cosmic self: one is located back in cosmic nature of Ātman. I would say Yājñavalkya's approach is very intellectual, cognitive-contemplative and apophasis-oriented whereas the older method of Śāṇḍilya was auto-suggestive, psychological, meditative, and cataphatic.

It is not the case that Yājñavalkya does not apply cataphatic methods. He does, for example, he says, Ātman is the omnipresent base on which everything is woven as warp and woof, everything is conceptualised or superimposed on that base. But any name, if fixed and formalised, will put the Ultimate in a certain perspective, and as such it would no more be the Ultimate. This applies to all terms used to denote the Ultimate such as Brahman, Puruṣa, and Ātman; or in English, God, the Ultimate etc. The scriptures describe the Ultimate as the pure essence of being, knowing, awareness, the infinity present in all, but any such description captures one or the other aspect or quality of its immanent expression. Therefore, after denying all attributed names and forms, the BĀU carefully presents 'the reality of reality / the truth of the truth' (*satyasya satyam*) as 'a way of naming' the Ultimate, the essence of everything. The truth can only be experienced in deep meditative state, but as soon as our mind conceptualises it and puts it in language it is not the same.

The Upaniṣads state cataphatically that Brahman is the self within all; it is awareness and bliss; it is Being/truth, awareness, and infinity (cf. TU 2.1.1,[22] BĀU III.4.1 and III.9.28), and also metaphorically they designate the Sun, the moon, the space, etc. as Brahman. All these positive descriptions are for the purpose of meditation on one or the other positive quality or majestic representation of Brahman, the Ultimate. For, in these forms the Ultimate is accessible to us and we can engage with it. Thus, the cataphatic approach is relational and contextual, and so can suggest only one aspect of the Ultimate, other aspects are shadowed. The Ultimate can be approached or venerated effectively, and in infinite individual ways, invoking one or the other name and form, but one needs to resort to ineffability and apophatic methods if one wants to awaken oneself to the all-accommodating nature of the Ultimate and feel his infinity. If one clings to any one particular form of the Ultimate and the name attached to that form, one is misled by an incomplete understanding or a wrong notion. Therefore, if one wants to understand the reality in its entirety, one must deny each of its fragmented identities or ap-

22 TU = *Taittirīya Upaniṣad.* See Limaye, *Eighteen Principal Upaniṣads*, 50–61; For a translation, see Olivelle, *The Early Upaniṣads*, 1998.

proximations. As soon as one realises this fact, thanks to this apophatic approach, all boundaries of specification collapse, and at that very moment the series of negations is automatically terminated. This makes one wake up and realise that one and the same truth is everywhere in the form of the essence of each entity, though it appears differently in different places. Thus, apophatic thinking leads the seeker to the highest state of understanding, where one will drop all fixed proper names and follow the ways of naming or describing the ultimate, such as 'the reality of reality' (cf. BĀU II.3.11) which cannot be easily formalised and fixed to one or the other aspect.

The BĀU formalises the apophatic method in the form of critical negation of *neti neti* (neither so nor so) as the best method of knowing the truth of the truth. As argued there, neither so nor so is there anything else beyond the Ultimate, that is the Sacred Fire in the ritual context and the ubiquitous Person/Self in the context of an inquiry about the essence of the world and Self. As the argument goes, however far or near, high or low, one may go, what one actually finds is the Ultimate but it remains concealed under its context-specific names and forms. If one does not negate these specific names and forms, one is unable to understand the complete truth. Thus, in earliest occurrences, the Upaniṣadic apophatic method highlighted the ultimacy of the Ultimate, one without anything beyond, but itself beyond all names, forms, and human quests. Thus, it taught that the Sacred/the Ultimate is beyond the named/known or nameable/knowable. But it also demonstrated that, thanks to its ubiquity, it is everywhere, here and now, but one can truly understand its ubiquity, only when one is awakened to its truth apophatically.

Once thus formalised and demonstrated through a dramatic discourse and applied multiple times in the BĀU, the apophatic method is regularly applied by other Upaniṣads of subsequent times.[23] Apophatic statements from the Upaniṣads describe the truth of the Ultimate, the purest essence, in the body and the universe, and also its experience. These apophatic statements are then coupled together with statements proclaiming the nondual unity of the Ultimate. The Original spirit of the apophatic teaching was holistic; every one-sided claim was critically negated, relativised, and adjusted as an aspect/face of the one all-pervasive whole.

In the system of Vedanta that elucidates the ideas of the Upaniṣads, the apophatic method is regarded as the accurate or the best method leading to the truth of Brahman,[24] the Ultimate, but mostly it is interpreted in the line of transcendentalism, and it is proclaimed that the Ultimate is that what remains at the pinnacle/

23 For details, see Acharya, "*Néti néti*," 4–5.

24 The early Upaniṣads, though they contain both cataphatic and apophatic statements, do not openly contract the two methods and name one or the other superior.

core of everything, without showing the reconciled whole. Beyond the Upaniṣads and the system of Vedānta, the apophatic thinking can be found embedded also in the Epic Sāṃkhya's concept of *avyakta*, the unmanifest, which refers to the source of everything, both consciousness and matter, in its primordial state. In any case, the concept of *avyakta*, the unmanifest that exists without name or form in the beginning of the creation, is apophatic in nature. No other Hindu school of thought discusses apophatic method of describing the ultimate. Rather, it is applied in transcendentalist and also pluralist relativist philosophies of the Buddhists and Jainas. Bhartṛhari (c. 5th century CE, philosophy of language) and Gauḍapāda (5/6th century, Vedanta) who draw on both Upaniṣadic as well as Buddhist sources apply apophatic method. In later centuries, the followers of the Buddhist, Jain, and Upaniṣadic Vedanta schools continue applying and refining apophatic methods.

In conclusion, let me state that apophatic methods are meant for exhausting the intellect and forcing it to see the truth holistically. To know that the ultimate is unknowable, at least intellectually, by way of definition, is the true knowing. As the BĀU 4.5.15 rhetorically puts, 'by what means would one know the knower!' (*vijñātāram are kena vijānīyāt*). The knower, the self, is the Ultimate himself, and he is the source of all knowing but himself remains beyond knowing. His attributes are knowable, describable but there are limits to the human mind/intellect; it cannot even enumerate all attributes. When one realises this fact and surrenders, the Ultimate Truth/God graciously reveals himself.

As Hindu traditions of all times teach, there are two main ways of experiencing the ultimate methodologically. The path of devotion is the first by surrendering oneself to the God in whichever form one is worshipping him, which begins with the practices of rites and rituals and culminates in self-surrender. This helps one to receive the grace of God and one is in the presence of God or in union with God eventually. Another way is the heroic path of training oneself through meditation to experience within oneself the all-present core seen as the Ultimate or God who is the sole actor, the sole being, in the world and beyond. In this way, one can directly experience the Ultimate or God within oneself but cannot know him and explain (cf. BĀU 3.4.1: *sākṣād aparokṣād brahma*), perhaps one can mystically smile and relax.

Diwakar Acharya is the Spalding Professor of Eastern Religions and Ethics at the University of Oxford, a fellow of All Souls College, and one of the senior editors of *St Andrews Encyclopedia of Theology*. He is an expert on Indian religions and philosophies and also Sanskrit literature. He has discovered rare Sanskrit and Prakrit texts from Nepalese manuscript archives, and published widely on topics which extend from the early Upaniṣads to philosophical systems, from early inscriptions to pre-modern documents and from poetry to ritual manuals.

Bibliography

Acharya, Diwakar. "*Néti néti*. Meaning and Function of an Enigmatic Phrase in the Gārgya-Ajātaśatru dialogue of *Bṛhad Āraṇyaka Upaniṣad* II.1 and II.3." *Indo-Iranian Journal* 56, no. 1 (January 2013): 3–39.

Acharya, Diwakar. "This World, in the Beginning, was Phenomenally Non-Existent: Āruṇi's Discourse on Cosmogony in the *Chāndogya Upaniṣad*." *Journal of Indian Philosophy* 44, no. 5 (November 2016): 833–64.

The Çatapatha-Brâhmaṇa in the Mâdhyandina-Çâkhâ with Extracts from the Commentaries of Sâyaṇa, Harisvâmin, and Dvivedagaṅga. Edited by Albrecht Weber. Leipzig: Otto Harrassowitz, 1924. Reprint of Berlin: 1855.

Colas, Gérard. "Evolution of Deism and Theism up to the 12th Century: Some Considerations." In *Viṣṇu-Nārāyaṇa: Changing Forms and the Becoming of a Deity in Indian Religious Traditions*, edited by Marcus Schmücker, 279–308. Vienna: Austrian Academy of Sciences, 2023.

Guha N., M. Dasti and S. Phillips. *God and the World's Arrangement: Readings from Vedanta and Nyaya Philosophy of Religion*. Indianapolis/Cambridge: Hackett Publishing Company, 2021.

Die Hymnen des Ṛigveda. Edited by Th. Aufrecht. 2 vols. Indische Studien 6–7. Berlin: Ferd. Dümmler's Verlagsbuchhandlung, 1861–3.

Keith, Arthur Berriedale. *The Religion and Philosophy of the Veda and Upanishads*. 2 vols. Harvard Oriental Series 31–32. Cambridge, MA: Harvard University Press, 1925. Reprint, Delhi: Motilal Banarsidass, 1970.

Limaye, V. P., and R. D. Vadekar. *Eighteen Principal Upaniṣads*. Poona: Vaidika Saṃśodhana Maṇḍala, 1958.

Olivelle, Patrick. *The Early Upaniṣads. Annotated Text and Translation*. Oxford: Oxford University Press, 1998.

Ram-Prasad, Chakravarthi 2023. "The Happiness that Qualifies Nonduality: Jñāna, Bhakti, and Sukha in Rāmānuja's Vedārthasaṃgraha", in *International Journal of Hindu Studies 27*, pp. 237–252.

The Rigveda: The Earliest Religious Poetry of India. Translated by Stephanie W. Jamison and Joel P. Brereton. 3 vols. Oxford: Oxford University Press, 2014.

Sarkar, Bihani. "Where Ants Dig up Gold: 'India', Selfhood and the Myths Manufacturing a Nation." In *British Academy Review* 30, (Summer 2017): 46–9.

Śrībhāṣya = Brahmasūtra-Śrībhāṣya of Sri Bhagavad Rāmānuja with the Śrutaprakāśikā of Śrī Sudarśanasūri, 2. vols. Chennai: Visishtadvaita Pracharini Sabha, 1989.

Vedārthasaṃgraha, ed. and trans. J. A. B van Buitenen. Poona: Deccan College Postgraduate and Research Institute, 1956.

Index

Ariyaratne, A. T. 29, 31, 35
Athanasius, St. 7
Augustine, St. 3, 7, 11
Aquinas, Thomas 7, 47, 53

Balthasar, Hans Urs von 11
Balzac, Honoré de 11–12
Bauer, Thomas 49
Blair, Hugh 2
Bodhi, Bhikku 29
Bonaparte, Napoleon 1
Bornkamm, Günther 10
Brereton, Joel 63
Bultmann, Rudolf 5
Butler, Joseph 4–5

Candrakīrti 24–27
Copleston, Frederick C. 47

Dalai Lama 31, 35
Descartes, René 1
Dewey, John 55
Dickens, Charles 12
Diderot, Denis 3–4

Elton, Geoffrey 6

Ferguson, Adam 2
Ford, David 55–57

Gadamer, Hans Georg 25
Gebarra, Ivone 22
Gibbon, Edward 2
Gross, Rita 29
Gutierrez, Gustavo 22

Hallaq, Wael 50, 52
Hanh, Thich Nhat 29, 31, 35
Hardy, Daniel 55
Harnack, Adolf von 8
Hayek, Friedrich 51
Herder, Johann Gottfried von 2
Hermann, Wilhelm 5
Hu, Hsiao Lan 29
Hume, David 2, 4
Hutcheson, Francis 2

Jackson, Sherman 49
Jacobs, Bill 1
Jamison, Stephanie 63
Jesus 1, 5, 7–11, 13
Johnson, Elizabeth 22

Kabilsingh, Chatsurman 29, 31, 35
Kant, Immanuel 4, 8, 50, 53
Kāṇva, Medhya 63
Käsemann, Ernst 10
Keith, Arthur 65
Kepnes, Steven 55
Khuankaew, Ouyporn 29
Klein, Anne 29
Küng, Hans 49

Leo XIII 2
Lessing, Gotthold 2–6, 17
Locke, John 51
Lopez, Donald 23–27
Loy, David 29
Loyola, Ignatius 5

Mahāghosananda 35
Maritain, Jacques 47
Mattson, Ingrid 49
McMahan, David 33
Meier, John P. 10
Mendelssohn, Moses 3
Metz, Johann Baptist 22
Moltmann, Jürgen 11

Newman, John Henry 6

Ochs, Peter 55, 56

Paley, William 3
Pannenberg, Wolfhart 9
Paul, St. 7
Peirce, John 55
Philoponus, Paul 53

https://doi.org/10.1515/9783111454658-005

Plato 4
Popper, Karl 51

Rahner, Karl 22
Rāmānuja 69
Rawls, John 51
Reimarus, H.S. 2
Renan, Auguste 8
Robertson, William 2
Römer, Thomas 14
Rousseau, Jean-Jacques 4
Rushd, Ibn (Averroes) 53

Said, Edward 52
Schweitzer, Albert 10
Schwöbel, Christoph 53, 56
Sivaraksa, Sulak 29, 31, 35
Smith, Adam 2
Smith, Mark 14
Strauss, David Friedrich 8

Tillich, Paul 5, 22
Troeltsch, Ernst 6
Tsomo, Karma Lekshe 29

Upton, Charles 49

Voltaire (François-Marie Arouet) 2–4

Walbridge, John 48
Watts, Isaac 17–18
Wesley, John 4–5
Winter, Tim 49, 56
Wright, Tom 10

www.ingramcontent.com/pod-product-compliance
Lightning Source LLC
Chambersburg PA
CBHW020131010526
44115CB00008B/1064